Make Poverty Business
Increase Profits and Reduce Risks
by Engaging with the Poor

Craig Wilson, an economist, was recently appointed as Executive Director of the Foundation for Development Co-operation in Australia. Immediately prior to accepting that appointment he worked with the International Finance Corporation, part of the World Bank Group, and was based for two years in Dhaka, Bangladesh, where he managed a programme aimed at improving investment climates in South Asia. He has extensive economic policy, development and business experience in developing countries worldwide. For five years to 2005 he consulted to the World Bank and numerous other international and private organisations. Much of this time was spent working on early economic policy in East Timor. Throughout the 1990s he served in the Australian diplomatic service and had long-term postings in Indonesia and Cambodia. He has a BA in economics from Griffith University, and a master's degree in economic policy from Columbia University. Along with Professor Emeritus George C. Lodge of Harvard Business School, he recently co-authored *A Corporate Solution to Global Poverty: How Multinationals Can Help the Poor and Invigorate Their Own Legitimacy*, published by Princeton University Press in May 2006.

Peter Wilson is a director of Libra Advisory Group Ltd, which advises governments and businesses on strategy and reform. He has lived or worked in a variety of developing and post-conflict countries including East Timor, Ethiopia, Indonesia, Kosovo and Sierra Leone. He is a former consultant with Strategos and McKinsey and has worked with a wide range of multinational clients including Danone, Masterfoods, Shell and two international banks. Throughout the 1990s he served in the British Diplomatic Service. He was, very briefly, UK press adviser for the boxing promoter Don King. He has a master's in Business Administration from INSEAD in France and a master's in Economics from the University of Oxford, where his research focused on the role of foreign direct investment in economic development. (Peter and Craig are not related.)

Make Poverty Business

Increase Profits and Reduce Risks by Engaging with the Poor

Craig Wilson and Peter Wilson

Routledge
Taylor & Francis Group

LONDON AND NEW YORK

In memory of Rory Harrigan, 1988–2006

With love to all the girls—Anita, Ava, Kate, Sacha, Sophie and Stella

First published 2006 by Greenleaf Publishing Ltd

Published 2017 by Routledge
2 Park Square, Milton Park, Abingdon, Oxon OX14 4RN
711 Third Avenue, New York, NY 10017, USA

Routledge is an imprint of the Taylor & Francis Group, an informa business

British Library Cataloguing in Publication Data:
A catalogue record for this book is available from the British Library.

ISBN: 978-1-874719-96-0 [hbk]

Contents

Acknowledgements

Many business people, officials, NGO workers and academics have, knowingly or unknowingly, given us ideas and evidence for this book. We are grateful to them all, and in particular to our various tutors at Columbia and Oxford Universities and INSEAD business school. They may be appalled that we are over-simplifying their complex work, but we feel that their ideas are too important to be left only to other specialists.

Rebekah Young at the World Business Council for Sustainable Development and Peter Brew at the International Business Leaders Forum gave us some excellent leads for case studies. Professor George Lodge at Harvard University Business School inspired us. George Pitcher, who combines the unusual roles of spin doctor and Church of England priest, has long given Peter ideas, moral backbone and vintage port when he's most needed them.

Of course all errors and omissions remain our own.

Preface

Poor people in developing countries could make excellent suppliers, employees and customers but are often ignored by major businesses. This omission leads to increased risk, higher costs and lower sales. Meanwhile, multinational corporations operating in developing countries are asked by governments and poverty activists to do more for economic development, but these exhortations are rarely based on a proper business case. In *Make Poverty Business* we try to bridge the gap by constructing a rigorous profit-making argument for multinational corporations to do more business with the poor. We aim to take economic development out of the corporate social responsibility ghetto and place it firmly in the core business interests of the corporation, and we argue that to see the poor only as potential consumers misses half of the story. The book should be read by international business managers seeking to increase profits and decrease risk in developing countries, and by development advocates who seek to harness the profit motive to reduce poverty.

We see the poor as much more than mere consumers at the 'bottom of the pyramid' and instead take a strategic view of all the ways in which a multinational company can interact with and influence the lives of the poor. The poor face poverty traps when they seek to deal with an international company. Based on sound economic theory and emerging good business practice, we recommend low-cost ways to overcome these traps and gain access to a larger and cheaper pool of employees and suppliers. The poor can also become a threat—to reputation and security—if relationships are badly managed. We believe that country risk is something that can be actively reduced through economic development rather than passively managed with lawyers and guards and we integrate concerns over political risk, legal failure and physical security into a business case for reducing poverty.

We argue that doing business with the poor can be profitably integrated into the core operations of *all* multinational companies, not only in those consumer manufacturers who see a marketing opportunity or those major corporations who feel under PR pressure to do some cosmetic corporate social responsibility. We make lots of low-risk, low-cost recommendations for specific activities. We examine the successes, failures and missed opportunities of a wide range of global companies including Wal-Mart, BP, Unilever, Shell and HSBC when dealing with the poor. And we discuss how to use a poverty perspective to provoke profitable innovation—not only to create new products and services but also to find new sources of competitive advantage in the supply chain and to develop more sustainable, lower-cost business models in developing countries.

We hope you enjoy the book. If you do, or even if you don't, please join the discussion at www.makepovertybusiness.com.

1

Introduction

(Not) talkin' 'bout a revolution

This book is about using an understanding of poverty to develop profitable business opportunities. There is no new paradigm here, no redefinition of the corporation, no need for a business revolution. Business people can go on serving their managers and their shareholders in the same way, seeking to make maximum profits at minimum risk. We follow Adam Smith when he says: 'It is not from the benevolence of the butcher, the brewer, or the baker, that we expect our dinner, but from their regard to their own interest',[1] but we also argue that by actively seeking to be benevolent we can sometimes identify new routes to satisfying our self-interest.

We make the simple claim that you will be a better international manager if you understand the dynamics of income, opportunity and wealth within your host country. Just as you would want to understand something about local law before signing a joint venture contract or something about local culture before you approve an advertising campaign, we believe that you should understand more about the lives of your customers, suppliers and employees before you do business with them. We assume you do not want to become an economist or a development guru, just as you don't want to be

---

1 *An Inquiry into the Nature and Causes of the Wealth of Nations* (1776).

a lawyer or a marketing expert. But you might feel that, if you know a bit more about these subjects, you'll understand better where your business is now, what risks it faces and what it could do to spend less and earn more in the future.

This is predominantly a book for business managers who want to increase their profits and reduce their risk. But we are not totally cold-hearted. We've written this book because we believe that, if we can incentivise you to think about the poor, then the poor will benefit. If you think the same, if you sometimes look through the plate glass windows of your hotel to the people beyond and you wonder what you can do for them, then so much the better. We hope this book will reassure you that you're already doing a lot, just by doing business, and give you some ideas for doing even more.

We're also writing this for people starting from the converse position, who want to help the poor and hope to use business as a tool to do so. If you work for a development organisation or a government and want to involve business in reducing poverty, we hope this book will help you to make the case to companies and to develop practical partnerships. If you can understand the concerns of business people and make cases for co-operation based on real-life examples and clear business incentives rather than moral exhortations, then surely you will be better at your job. With all the talk of corporate social responsibility, licences to operate and the moral responsibilities of business, it is easy to forget that business people don't have total freedom to follow your ideas and indeed have a legal responsibility to serve the best interests of their shareholders before anyone else. But we believe there are some areas where their interests and yours converge, and this book is about identifying and developing them.

> ⁕⁕ Most academics, policy-makers and development agency professionals endeavouring to catalyse pro-poor enterprise don't have real business-based experience to draw on. Their knowledge of how markets operate and the problems faced by business of all kinds is largely theoretical or conceptual.
>
> Thus they operate on the basis of many partially informed and often downright incorrect assumptions about markets and enterprise. This means the policies and interventions they design and implement, with the best intentions, to catalyse the efficient operation of markets or the creation of enterprise just don't work or don't work nearly well enough. ⁕⁕
>
> Source: *Enterprise Solutions to Poverty*, Shell Foundation, March 2005 (www.shellfoundation.org/download/download.html, 20 March 2006).

Just as we say that poverty alleviation is only one element of deciding a business strategy, we also say that business and the profit motive is just one part of development. There are many things in development that a business can't, won't or shouldn't do, but we're choosing to focus on those areas where the profit motive can be harnessed to satisfy development aims.

During our careers, we've moved around between all these approaches. Between us, we've worked as government officials, development and political advisers, business strategy consultants and entrepreneurs (we hope this variety doesn't mean that we weren't any good at any of them). We've lived or worked in many of the most interesting and difficult countries in the world including Iraq, Afghanistan, East Timor, Indonesia, Papua New Guinea, Sierra Leone, Ethiopia, Bangladesh, Kosovo and Vietnam—so we hope our ideas aren't too naive or Western-centric.

Bottom of the pyramid

Sadly, it might seem like we've been beaten to it. C.K. Prahalad's book *The Fortune at the Bottom of the Pyramid: Eradicating Poverty through Profits*[2] has already set the agenda, with endorsements by Bill Gates and appearances on best-seller lists all over the world. If we weren't so publicly committed to ethical business, we'd probably have him shot. You'd be well advised to read his book before starting on ours because he does the motivation, the ambition and the shining city on the hill. We're more interested in replacing a few light bulbs down here in the valley.

The 'bottom of the pyramid' is, in essence, a marketing approach and refers to targeting the mass markets of the poor and supplying them with better and cheaper products. For example, instead of selling shampoo in large bottles for $3, a business should sell shampoo in small sachets for 10 cents—thus acknowledging that poor people can't tie up capital in (for them) large purchases. There is nothing wrong with this. But marketing to the poor is not new. Coca-Cola, for example, is excellent at it and has been for a long time.

---

2 Published by Wharton School of Publishing (University of Pennsylvania) in 2004.

The real challenge is helping those same poor people get a job, making that job sustainable, and creating access to savings, credit, insurance and the other features of a developed economy while linking this to the mainstream profit-making operations of business.

We also have a fear that is driven by our experience of that last big trend in business strategy—innovation. Our concern is that doing new things for the poor is, in effect, a special case of general business innovation and may suffer from the same weaknesses.

We all know what the guru cycle looks like. A couple of books are published about companies that are currently doing well and the authors imply that this is because the company is following some of the authors' own ideas (here we recall that Enron was widely praised for its approach to innovation during the 1990s boom time and boo.com won an award from Bain management consultants shortly before going spectacularly bust). Based on a limited number of examples, authors call for wholesale reinvention of business practices and culture with nothing less than total commitment required. A few companies try out the new paradigm at major expense in terms of time and money, but don't have the luck or skill to pull off a major success. They get bored, disillusioned or impatient, and move on to some different initiative. Meanwhile, a few of the initial exciting examples run into the ground or some other explanation is invented for the success of the companies in the case studies. The agenda is discredited and the caravan moves on.

We do use a few case studies in this book, but mostly for the rhetorical value of illustrating our points or provoking ideas. We do not make the unscientific implication based on a single study at a single point in time that the example we've chosen is responsible for the company's success or that the example will continue to be successful in five years' time. Most importantly, we do not offer any single set of recommendations or any single explanation for a company's success.

In our experience, most companies face no shortage of profitable opportunities or potentially valuable initiatives. With limited management resources, the challenge is to choose between them. Most companies can take only one or two major initiatives at a time and, if this year is cost-cutting, then alleviating poverty will just have to wait for a while. And a company certainly can't chase every possible new product idea or new group of customers just because books written with no knowledge of the reader's specific circumstances think they might be profitable.

So there are no major initiatives in this book and no calls for wholesale change. Instead, we hope that a manager who reads this book and then starts talking to a wider range of people and reading from a wider range of sources will start to make slightly better day-to-day decisions. The book should prompt more networking, more curiosity and more analysis. It is these activities, specific to the manager and the company's circumstances, which should then form the basis for business decisions, rather than a bandwagon of books and conferences.

When managers start following this prescription, their bosses may not even know the reason why but they might start spotting lower costs, higher sales, better local relationships and less fire-fighting. Over time, the ideas might spread and start becoming a standard part of a manager's toolkit. Then none of us will need to cross our fingers that our limited number of high-profile case studies will continue to prove successful.

A wider view of poverty

When thinking about poverty, we've tried to think like carbon-based life forms rather than economists. Many of the problems that affect poor people are not directly related to what they can or cannot purchase in the market. Like the rest of us, poor people worry most about lack of control over their own lives. They want choice about where and how they work. They're disproportionately subject to abuse by security forces or petty officials. They have little say about the activities of the government, aid agencies and businesses in their area. They're denied access to public services. As a result, many of the things that could improve poor people's lives will not take the form of market transactions and will not show up in economic statistics.

If this all sounds obvious, then you'll be pleased to know that economists and aid agencies are finally latching on to it. Prompted by a major World Bank report, *Voices of the Poor*,[3] which for the first time made a systematic survey of poor people's own opinions, many development professionals are thinking far harder about questions of security and autonomy for poor people as well as income and economic opportunity. Some of the most interesting company initiatives in the field of poverty alleviation are not about selling people more things, but co-operating with the local community to increase autonomy and provide mutual security.

3 World Bank, *Voices of the Poor: Can Anyone Hear Us?* (New York: Oxford University Press for the World Bank, 1999; www1.worldbank.org/prem/poverty/voices/reports.htm, 20 March 2006).

Even if we restrict ourselves to economic issues, the important problems can be solved in a wider range of ways than just giving poor people more money, better training or cheaper goods. Many poor people can't offer themselves to the job market because they lack information and contacts rather than skills. Many potential entrepreneurs have trouble proving collateral and gaining access to credit, and so can't build up a business to be large enough to operate at an efficient scale. Even when they do have access to credit, if they do not have access to insurance or other forms of risk-sharing, then credit availability dramatically increases their risks. Poor people often face huge fluctuations in living standards caused by environmental disasters, conflict or political change, and it is these risks that are important to people rather than an average of their income over time.

It is precisely this complexity of poverty that offers the opportunity. If we see poverty only as wages and prices, it is difficult to escape the conflict that companies want lower wages and higher prices, and poor people want the opposite. But, if a company can expand its potential workforce by offering information and overcoming discrimination or can develop efficient local suppliers by helping them secure credit, then both sides will benefit. What's more, by understanding and influencing the priorities of aid agencies, a company can often call on development resources to undertake those actions that have the least obvious business case or that require unfamiliar skills, leaving the company to focus on those areas that are closest to their current business concerns and capabilities. Companies can play huge roles as catalysts, advocates, problem-solvers and conveners long before they have to spend any money.

°°Our experience as a donor operating alongside a major multinational has convinced us that big companies possess a wide-ranging set of tangible and intangible 'assets' that can be of huge value in the fight against poverty, especially via an enterprise-focused attack. So we consciously and transparently seek to deploy these assets in support of our work and that of our external partners wherever we can.

The 'assets' we are referring to fall into three categories:

First and most fundamentally, established business is a vast repository of generalised business skills that are encapsulated in people, knowledge and techniques . . .

The second asset category falls under the heading of 'convening power'. This is shorthand for the subtle and overt ways by which a company's track record, reputation, brand, political reach and financial clout makes other people listen and respond to what the company has to say.

And the third category includes the [Shell] company and sector-specific physical and market knowledge-based assets that lie at the core of the unique processes of value creation and capture on which every company relies.

Usually, all these asset classes are fully and properly deployed in the interests of the business and its shareholders. And when business operates well in developing countries, this is a huge source of social value via jobs created, taxes paid, technology transferred, and so on. But typically these are not the assets multinational companies offer, or are asked to use, in order to discharge their corporate social responsibility or sustainable development commitments.

What our experience suggests is that deployment of these private value-creating assets via pro-poor enterprise interventions, could offer a huge but still unrealised contribution to the efforts of the international development community and poor countries to make poverty history. **

Source: *Enterprise Solutions to Poverty*, Shell Foundation, March 2005 (www.shellfoundation.org/download/download.html, 20 March 2006).

Going native—stumbling across the poverty perspective

We once worked with a multinational company whose operations in an Eastern European country were heading into difficulties. Their fast-moving consumer goods were becoming decidedly slow-moving despite a strong international brand, highly trained expatriate managers and an impressive track record of establishing new operations in emerging markets.

Turnover was down, margins were down and costs were rising. Some of the managers advocated price cuts in the interests of turnover, others wanted to defend their margins and the company's quality reputation by maintaining or even increasing prices. In the absence of any real under-standing of the causes of the problem, neither of these options was very convincing and the debate soon descended into personal rancour. Arguments were won on the basis of charisma and power rather than evidence, and the losers soon resigned or were sacked. Meanwhile, head office showed little interest in the details, but complained at the declining headline figures in their outpost's monthly reports.

We were called in to 'do' innovation which, at that time, was considered the solution to all corporate problems. But, while trying to find some interesting new products for the company, we stumbled on a much more fundamental problem.

As part of our innovation project, we encouraged a cross-section of the company's local and expatriate managers to talk to as wide a range as possible of local people. We offered prizes for reports of conversations with the oldest and the youngest, the richest and the poorest, the most sophisticated urbanite and the person who lived furthest from the capital city. We encouraged the team to have interesting conversations about people's lives rather than ask boring questions about their attitudes to fast-moving consumer goods. No subject was out of bounds, and we created an atmosphere where people would want to return to the team with interesting stories and emerging hypotheses rather than with statistically significant data.

We should make clear that we hadn't yet jumped on the poverty bandwagon and were not doing this because we thought the company should have any interest in politics, poverty or development. We simply wanted to prompt the team to have some understanding of the people they were trying to sell to and to break them out of their insularity. We got bored with asking 'what does quality mean?' and being answered with a list of technical indicators that were meaningless to anyone outside the company. We thought it might be a good idea for people to start talking to their grandmothers, children and friends, and we thought that they could come up with new ideas only if they first had some new experiences and information. There was no great science in any of this and, with the exception of our huge fees, it didn't cost the company very much.

Quite unexpectedly, the reports that emerged not only prompted some ideas for new products and services, but also contained the crucial clues on where the existing business was going wrong. The team came back with a story of a society and economy in flux, in which attitudes to international companies were changing and the competitive environment was moving against expensive multinationals. We ended up pursuing some quite odd questions such as the effect of the country's forthcoming membership of the European Union on the incomes of farmers. We couldn't have predicted these issues in advance and they were well outside our initial brief. We could not have analysed them using conventional market research because we would not even have known what questions to ask.

The story seemed to go something like this. When the country opened up after Communism, international companies were seen as an unequivocally good thing. They brought quality, glamour and reliability. In particular, international quality actually meant something, because local products were likely to kill you. The competitive environment was particularly benign because local competitors were alarmingly incompetent. The economy was too immature to support much outsourcing and only a fully integrated company could deliver reliable goods. This required international managers and expensive systems, and our multinational was uniquely well placed to provide this. Our client benefited from an effective monopoly as the only reliable supplier in the country, and the group's business model of transplanting their Western European experience and systems to Eastern Europe was reaping impressive results.

Now move on ten years to the time of our project. 'International' was no longer synonymous with 'good'. Some of the promised gains of capitalism hadn't emerged and there was growing concern with the inequality caused by economic freedom. Foreign companies were seen as exploiters rather than liberators. The forthcoming membership of the European Union seemed set to make matters even worse by threatening groups of people such as peasant farmers who were important to the national psyche. In these changing times, people harked back to products that they remembered as kids or associated with their home regions, and became better at questioning the clever messages of mass advertising and international branding. Some of these feelings were based on prejudice and fear, and were perhaps plain wrong, but they had a real effect on people's willingness to trust even the best of the international companies.

Perhaps none of this would have mattered if our client could have continued to rely on its de facto monopoly over quality goods, but these subjective issues in society were combined with some real changes in the competitive environment and the company found itself squeezed by some increasingly competent local players. The economy had matured around them without them noticing and, at the bottom of the market, local companies without the high costs of expatriate managers and smart offices could now produce quality low-cost products that would no longer kill you. At the top end of the market, niche players could concentrate on product design and marketing based on real local understanding, and outsource everything else to a growing network of reliable local suppliers and distributors. Our client was left in the classically disastrous position of being neither low-cost nor perceived as high-quality. In addition, the company had to support a high-cost, fully integrated infrastructure with a customer base that no longer wanted or needed to buy its products. The fact that the company had contributed to the economic development that allowed all this to happen provided scant comfort.

This looked like a pretty good set of conclusions from a few chats with our team members' grannies. We decided to check out this story—and get a paid holiday—by taking the team to Spain. In the 1970s, Spain had emerged from its period of isolation and we thought its experience would provide some signposts for what could happen in Eastern Europe. Sure enough, we found a country that had initially seen international companies as the source of all good things, but over time had developed the scepticism and self-confidence to start favouring authentic local experiences over internationally imported products. Local companies had emerged that were equally as competent as the internationals, but knew more about the country. We noted that the most successful fast-food joints were neither traditional tapas bars (too dirty and unreliable) nor McDonald's (too bland and foreign), but modern tapas restaurants that combined local traditions with international quality control. Our hypotheses were complete and we invented a trite slogan to represent our client's desired new profile along the lines of 'the local company that's better than the multinationals'.

Our client found the conclusions frightening, but credible. The company realised that its expatriate mind-set had led it to concentrate on all the wrong issues, such as how price indicated quality, while ignoring factors such as its own nationality that were irrelevant at home but crucial abroad.

It also realised that it had some underrated strengths that it could use to respond to this new mood in the host country. It found a hidden saviour in its procurement manager, a decidedly unglamorous local woman who rarely spoke up at meetings dominated by noisy expats with marketing degrees but who had quietly spent her time developing the skills of a network of local suppliers. The company's image, unwittingly reinforced by its own advertising, was of a rootless international company with no local links; but all the time they'd been one of the prime movers behind the increasing prosperity of local farmers and other small-scale suppliers. Its first move was to change all its advertising and branding to highlight this fact. And (we hope) they started paying the procurement manager as much as they paid the expats.

We seemed to have stumbled across a common problem for multinational companies operating in emerging economies. When our client first entered the country, it had little choice but to set up an expensive, fully integrated operation run by expensive expatriates—as the economic infrastructure simply didn't exist to support any other type of operation. But over a relatively short period of time the economy developed, partly thanks to the company's presence and partly to its benefit in terms of higher spending power and a larger market. What was missing was a migration plan to respond to the opportunities for cost-cutting, outsourcing and localisation in this maturing economy and an understanding of what the rise of local competitors would mean for the business. There was even less comprehension of how local people misunderstood their operation and resented them as opportunistic outsiders, and little idea of how slick global branding only contributed to the problem.

The expatriate managers not only followed our plans by putting a much greater emphasis on local talent and launching a series of local products with identifiable local links, they also took their message back to head office. They argued that its role in an under-developed economy was rightly as a provider of management, blueprints and systems. But, over time, country managers' specific job should be to develop a uniquely local operation, deeply embedded in the host economy. Head office's role should then be as a clearinghouse to spread products, ideas and good practice around the autonomous local units, rather than acting to maintain a series of standardised, high-cost operations that were rapidly losing their reason for existing.

Head office told them to go back and produce some results before getting too cocky. That process is now under way.

There may not be much new in this in theory, even if we continue to see companies make the same old mistakes in practice. Companies have long understood the advantages of outsourcing and indigenous labour. Locally tailored advertising of global brands is familiar, albeit not often backed up by genuine localisation of products and operations.

What might be new is the use of a poverty perspective as one tool to help identify and solve the problems. Country managers often complain to head office that they simply can't find sufficiently competent local staff and suppliers, and so have to rely on expensive imports and integrated operations. Well, poverty experts have thought about these problems from the perspective of those local people who can't persuade you to give them a job or a contract, and it makes sense to steal some of their existing analysis on poverty traps. We do so later in the book. Similarly, if you can understand the effect you are having on economic development and poverty, and identify hidden gems like some existing procurement good practice, then you will find it far easier to gain the support of governments, development agencies and local people for your operations and your localised marketing will be far more credible. You'd be surprised at how people are willing to support your self-interested efforts to develop competent local staff and suppliers once you've learned the 'development-speak' vocabulary to describe what you're up to.

If we were going into this company now, knowing what we know about poverty, we could have taken a few short cuts. We would have commissioned an economist to understand the economic benefits of the company's presence in the country and used this to underpin a credible communications campaign. We would also have used the analysis to identify the changes in the competitive environment. Were the beneficial changes being driven by our company and other multinationals creating a different type of economy that offered different opportunities and different competitive challenges? Finally, we would have used an understanding of poverty traps to deal with this changing environment, sign mutually beneficial deals with local people and steal a march on local and international competitors.

We've deliberately started this story a long way from poverty, as we wanted to root what we say in the day-to-day concerns of business people who are under such pressure from head office for poor monthly sales figures that they have little time to worry about anything else. We hope we've shown that a better understanding of the economy and society in which they were operating would have helped the company to identify the emerging problems in its business model and its corporate image. We'll go on to argue that some of the tools of poverty analysis could then have helped them solve the problems by identifying how best to trade with local people.

But, from our other perspective of the person primarily interested in poverty reduction, why should we care about this? Isn't it this all a rather grubby matter of corporate strategy? Well, emerging evidence shows that the benefit to an economy of a foreign investor depends crucially on the number of ties it has with local companies and employees.

The mere presence of a self-contained expatriate enclave with no local suppliers has little effect on the productivity of local companies and plays no role in technology transfer. However, local companies that directly supply a multinational company (MNC) show significant increases in productivity. The benefits of foreign investment do not happen simply through a spillover effect in which local companies are incentivised to copy MNCs' technology from afar, but instead through transfer of a complex culture of behaviour, practices and technology that can be transmitted only through direct business relationships.[4] The more direct business relationships there are, the more the local economy benefits.

4   For the basic argument on the economic benefits of direct business contact and the importance of tacit business knowledge, see Sanjaya Lall, *Competitiveness, Skills and*

°°Linkages offer benefits to foreign affiliates and domestic suppliers, as well as to the economy in which they are forged as a whole. For foreign affiliates, local procurement can lower production costs in host economies with lower costs and allow greater specialization and flexibility, with better adaptation of technologies and products to local conditions. The presence of technologically advanced suppliers can provide affiliates with access to external technological and skill resources, feeding into their own innovative efforts. The direct effect of linkages on domestic suppliers is generally a rise in their output and employment. Linkages can also transmit knowledge and skills between the linked firms. A dense network of linkages can promote production efficiency, productivity growth, technological and managerial capabilities and market diversification for the firms involved. Finally, for a host economy as a whole, linkages can stimulate economic activity and, where local inputs substitute for imported ones, benefit the balance of payments. The strengthening of suppliers can in turn lead to spillovers to the rest of the host economy and contribute to a vibrant enterprise sector.°°

Source: UN Conference on Trade and Development, *World Investment Report 2001: Promoting Linkages* (Geneva: United Nations Publications, 2001).

There's one more link we need to make before we can convincingly argue that curing our fast-moving consumer goods (FMCG) company's travails would also contribute to reducing poverty. We've talked about the impact of local linkages on economic growth, but does economic growth through foreign investment automatically reduce poverty or do the spoils just accrue to people who are already rich? This is a huge economic issue with plenty of conflicting evidence, and later we'll discuss how it can be in a company's interest to explicitly seek business relationships with people who are currently excluded from economic opportunity. But, for now, we think our for-

Technology (Cheltenham, UK: Edward Elgar, 2001). For specific research on direct business relationships versus generalised spillover effects, see: E.-G. Lim, *Determinants of, and the Relation between, Foreign Direct Investment and Growth: A Summary of the Recent Literature*, IMF Working Paper WP/01/175, November 2001; B. Smarzynska, *Does Foreign Investment Increase the Productivity of Domestic Firms? In Search of Spillovers through Backward Linkages* (Washington, DC: World Bank, September 2002); and M. Blomstrom and E. Wolff, 'Multinational Corporations and Productivity Convergence in Mexico', in W. Baumol, R. Nelson and E. Wolff (eds.), *Convergence of Productivity: Cross-national Studies and Historical Evidence* (Oxford: Oxford University Press, 1994): ch. 10.

mer economics tutor, Dr Marcel Fafchamps at Oxford University, has it about right:

> After examining essentially all the explanations that have been proposed to account for differences in prosperity levels between countries and regions, I conclude that . . . the key to catching-up is to copy and absorb technological improvements invented elsewhere and to emulate advanced economies . . . I acknowledge that understanding what is responsible for growth is far from exhausting the larger question of economic development. For instance, it is often believed that growth exacerbates income inequalities and may even have perverse effects on certain vulnerable groups. To attain economic development, it is argued, one must achieve 'not just growth' in aggregate output but also its equitable distribution among various segments of society. Yet, while it is true that the redistribution of the new prosperity generated by growth is far from automatic, there must be something to redistribute before we can talk of redistributing anything. Over the last two decades, slow growth has been Africa's main problem, not the unequal distribution of increases in prosperity, which have been small by most accounts.[5]

And, of course, we must remember our point that poverty is not only about level of income. Foreign companies can also offer autonomy, self-respect and security to the poor people they do business with. We will discuss all of this in the pages ahead.

•• The UN's Commission on the Private Sector and Development recently released a report that, a few hundred years after Adam Smith came to a similar conclusion, finally acknowledged that 'the savings, investment and innovation that lead to development are undertaken largely by private individuals, corporations and communities.'

It concluded that developing countries' governments must find better ways to foster private industry, especially the forgotten medium-sized enterprises. While obvious to many, it marked the culmination of a remarkable change of heart for the UN.

5 Marcel Fafchamps, 'Engines of Growth and Africa's Economic Performance', July 2000; www.economics.ox.ac.uk/members/marcel.fafchamps/homepage/engines.pdf, 24 May 2006.

The report may also herald a new phase in development policy after the macro-economic reforms of the 1990s failed to reap the hoped-for results. 'A lot of developing country governments have spent the last ten years restructuring their public sectors: and suddenly are looking over the edge of the road,' says Mark Malloch Brown, head of the UN Development Programme.

'What's missing is jobs and growth. There is no sign of an emerging tax base to sustain services in the future. Why not? There's a remarkably thin middle.' The UNDP and others believe that multinationals can play a crucial role in fostering this 'middle', the small and medium enterprises, through support for local suppliers—with the added benefit that local people may show an interest in seeing them stick around. "

Source: Financial Times, 24 June 2004.

" Development institutions and developing countries are beginning to recognise the basic structure of global development finance is probably not going to change. Public sector development assistance is between Dollars 50bn and Dollars 60bn; while the private sector offers between Dollars 200bn and Dollars 300bn in cross-border flows. "

Source: Joseph O'Keefe, Director of Corporate Relations, International Finance Corporation, quoted in the Financial Times, 24 June 2004.

Not corporate social responsibility

We dislike the term 'corporate social responsibility' (CSR) and we dislike the way it's developed as a separate discipline from business management. Our interest is in running the core business more profitably and in doing so play-ing a role in poverty alleviation.

It is not about apologising for your profits with glossy brochures or ran-dom acts of philanthropy in a programme managed by a group of specialists who are only tenuously connected to the core business. It isn't about meet-ing standards, achieving best practice or ticking a series of compliance boxes, but about innovating to find new ways of dealing with the poor in order to create new sources of competitive advantage. If you do all of this properly, you'll want to keep it secret and not publicise it in indistinguish-able corporate advertisements on CNN (Cable News Network).

""At the heart of the issue lies pressure from those NGOs to whom modern capitalism and profit-making are anathema. They have been remarkably successful at gaining the moral high ground (they are even dubbed a 'civil society') and in nurturing a distrust of business. This in turn has led business to distrust itself, producing a climate in which companies rush to embrace all aspects of the CSR agenda. The challenge now is to generate a new climate where business considers what the right elements to pursue under the heading of 'good management' are. If that cannot be achieved, more regulation will inevitably move the equation from good management, within the control of business, to pernicious and delusional CSR.""

Source: Letter from Patricia Peter, Institute of Directors, to *The Economist*, 5 February 2005.

Most importantly, we find phrases such as 'responsibility' and 'licence to operate' mildly sinister, as they imply that there is widespread consensus about the correct way for a company to behave and the only question is then whether the company will be good enough to comply. But every society has huge questions about the balance between economic growth and the environment, or the trade-offs between high standards for the employed and opportunity for the unemployed. It is not for self-appointed CSR experts to prejudge what decisions a society or a business should make about these complex questions. There are obviously basic standards of legality and ethics that we might all agree on and that we would want all companies to adhere to. But, after that, a company's job is to get on with its business at some acceptable point on the spectrum—not try to converge on some single point that will make outsiders happy but may ultimately be damaging for its employees, customers or suppliers.

This is not to say that all the activities currently conducted under the heading of CSR are wrong and should be stopped, but simply that we should be much more rigorous about the business case and not be ashamed to talk about the core business and profits as the real sources of value to society.

As an example of why this matters, consider the case of Western oil com-panies and their fear of 'asymmetric competition'. Oil companies spend most of their time worrying about the emergence of national oil companies from countries such as China, Russia and Saudi Arabia, which are increas-ingly seeking business in countries other than their home base. Unencumbered by pressure from a picky Western consumer base to pursue CSR and subject to much less regulation, they can save a fortune on social development and public affairs experts and get on with the simple job of digging up oil.

If all we do is impose unprofitable but nice CSR activities on the Western companies that are susceptible to consumer pressure but without a thought for their ability to create value, we will not only put the nice amenable companies out of business, we'll also be missing opportunities for economic growth. Our recommendations should be so clearly rooted in a business case that even those asymmetric competitors will want to adopt them. Whether we like it or not, in a globalising world our ability to impose CSR through Western consumer pressure and government regulation, as opposed to through the profit motive, is set to decline.

The following quotes about outsourcing of Western jobs to India indicate the slipperiness of corporate social responsibility as a guide to ethical and profitable decision-making and the danger for companies in embracing a loosely defined concept that can be turned against them.

" Campaigners are using the enormous buying power of the student market to put pressure on companies who ignore corporate social responsibility when they offshore jobs to India.

Finance union Amicus and the National Union of Students (NUS) are launching a national campaign to assert themselves as stakeholder organisations for companies using CSR as a public relations tool.

Amicus and NUS represent over four million individual members and both have traditions of strong campaigning on global ethics. Amicus is currently campaigning for Corporate Social Responsibility programmes, available to UK insurance and banking workers, to be extended to the Indian operations of UK companies. Indian workers suffer from dignity at work issues and are denied the right to union membership. They are often forced to change their accents and study *Eastenders* and UK football scores to mask the fact they are based in India . . . Corporate Social Responsibility is a major PR tool for any high street name you can think of. Our research is showing that they can expect their brands to be damaged if they make bad CSR decisions regarding their offshore workforce. *CSR fails when the public gets a whiff of hypocrisy.*"

Source: www.amicustheunion.org

It appears that CSR is an uncontroversial concept aimed at raising standards for everyone, albeit a double-edged tool for companies that don't get it exactly right. We might quibble at the seriousness of being 'forced' to watch *Eastenders* as a form of human rights abuse, and remind ourselves that presumably people work for these companies because it's better than the available alternatives. But Amicus's heart seems to be in the right place and they have Indian interests in mind.

Now let's look at another statement by Amicus on the decision of a specific company, Aviva, to outsource from the UK to India.

Dave Fleming, national officer of trade union Amicus, said: 'This deplorable announcement by Aviva is based purely on greed. It ignores Aviva's corporate social responsibility towards its UK employees and customers because company turnover is overwhelmingly UK-based'. He added: 'They are throwing thousands of families on to the scrap-heap for a 40 per cent saving that will not be passed on to their customers.'

Amicus called on the company to reverse the 'despicable' decision and said the union would back workers in 'whatever course of action' they choose to take.

Source: www.amicustheunion.org

Perhaps CSR is actually about defending existing UK jobs at the expense of potential Indian ones.

India's $1.5 billion outsourcing business illustrates how foreign investment and trade have benefited the country . . . By 2008, it is expected to attract one-third of all foreign direct investment and generate $60 billion per year in exports, creating nearly a million new jobs in the process . . . Consumers benefit from lower prices, better quality and a wider selection of products and services. Domestic demand has also soared in response to these lower prices.

Without early investments by multinational companies, the outsourcing industry probably would never have emerged. Pioneers such as British Airways and General Electric were among the first to see the opportunity to move IT and other back-office operations to India. The success of these companies demonstrated to the world that the country was a credible offshoring destination. The multinationals also trained thousands of local workers, many of whom transferred their skills to Indian companies that arose in response. **"**

Source: Diana Farrell and Adil S. Zainulbhai, 'A Richer Future for India', *McKinsey Quarterly*, 13 December 2004: 50-59.

Can the fuzzy notion of CSR tell you what's right and what's wrong in this case? Are British Airways, Aviva and General Electric the heroes or the villains in this story?

Perhaps even thinking in these moralistic terms is unhelpful. The companies don't seem to have done anything illegal or unethical, and nobody forces us to buy from them or work for them. They're increasing our range of options and experimenting with new ways of working, with the long-term benefits being difficult to measure or predict. The static idea of CSR, or a stakeholder analysis, would have immediately identified the disadvantages to the current UK workers long before the advantages to Indian workers, business people and consumers became measurable or obvious.

These thoughts on outsourcing to India provides some signposts to our overall approach. We doubt that the companies involved thought much about poverty alleviation but, if they'd explicitly included it in their brainstorming sessions, it might have sparked the outsourcing notion much sooner. They then had to take a risk to do something that now seems entirely obvious and had to learn to work with people that many global companies had long dismissed as too incompetent or poor to be of interest.

The outsourcing pioneers had to withstand criticism from people who were distorting the companies' own CSR vocabulary to protect their narrow interests. An explicit understanding of poverty would have allowed the companies to understand the benefits they were bringing to the country and to make a strong economic and ethical case that might well have shown up their critics as selfish and rather silly.

In short, an understanding of poverty might have helped them come up with the idea, implement it effectively and manage the risks. That is what this book is all about.

Follow-up questions

What opportunities to increase profits or cut costs would arise if you consciously sought to help the poor?

What do local people in government, the media and the grassroots think about your operations? Does it matter? Could you communicate with them differently?

What forms of global corporate reputation are important to you? Could you improve your reputation and defuse criticism if you understood and could communicate your impact on the poor?

How much do you know about how your host economy is changing? Do you have a migration plan to deal with these changes? What elements of your business model will be redundant in ten years' time? What competitive pressures will you be under? What are you doing to prepare?

Further reading

Empires of Profit: Commerce, Conquest and Corporate Responsibility by Daniel Litvin, published by Texere (London and New York) in 2003, gives cautionary tales from four centuries of attempts by Western companies to operate effectively abroad. Case studies include: Nike's attempts to practise corporate social responsibility in its factories in Asia; Shell's problems handling protests and attacks in Nigeria; and Rupert Murdoch's efforts to adapt to local politics and culture in China and India.

Inevitable Surprises: A Survival Guide for the 21st Century by Peter Schwartz, published in London by Free Press in 2003, outlines the political, social, economic and environmental changes that your company should be preparing for. Schwartz is the former head of Shell's famous scenario planning team and brings out the business implications of current trends.

'Localization: The Revolution in Consumer Markets', by Darrell Rigby and Vijay Vishwanath in *Harvard Business Review*, April 2006, makes the case for much greater localisation of consumer products. As of 24 April 2006 it was available for paid download at http://harvardbusinessonline.hbsp.harvard.edu.

For links to these resources and other relevant material, go to www.makepovertybusiness.com

2

What business can and can't do for the poor

There has been a lot of confusion about what business can do for the poor. Faced with the failure of many development projects and the relatively small size of aid budgets, many development practitioners have started to hope that businesses can do almost everything. They have been strengthened in this view by the advent of corporate social responsibility (CSR), which they imagine will allow them to persuade businesses to do all sorts of morally good things, regardless of the business case.

In the previous chapter, we foreshadowed our scepticism about CSR as a way of benefiting the poor. We criticised it from a business perspective as we see it as stifling innovation and creating a distraction from the real business of creating value. In Chapter 9 on reputation we discuss how profit, rather than any other measure of corporate activity, is the best first estimate of how much value a business creates for society and that we should therefore encourage businesses to make profit rather than try to distract them with other tasks.

In this chapter, we'll try to learn from the people who oppose CSR from the developmental perspective. We don't always agree with their underlying philosophy because they often argue that CSR 'add-ons' do little for poverty

alleviation and therefore that business as a whole does little for development—missing the point that it is the core business not the add-ons that
create the real developmental value. But their criticisms of specific CSR
activities and, in particular, the tendency of businesses to become involved
in development programmes unconnected to their core business are important and give us extra reasons to be sceptical about CSR as a whole.

So we'll outline the emerging developmental criticisms of CSR. We'll
emphasise that businesses *cannot* do everything in development and that CSR
will do little to change that. Then we'll describe the fundamentals of what
we think businesses *can* do. Finally, we'll discuss how all this works on a
global scale and, in particular, why many countries may miss out on the
benefits of international business activity.

What businesses can't do for the poor

Under the rubric of CSR, some companies are getting directly involved in
development programmes unrelated to the core business such as building
schools and hospitals in their host communities. Jedrzej George Frynas has
studied such behaviour by multinational oil companies in Africa and come
to some depressing conclusions about the *capability* and *incentives* of oil companies to implement development programmes properly (see box).

" Shell's main Nigerian affiliate, Shell Petroleum Development Company
(SPDC), provides its major contract managers with a development budget so
that, when a new pipeline is built, the manager can initiate a new
development project within a community in order to enable pipeline
construction to continue unhindered. When the SPDC team finishes the
construction of a particular section of the pipeline, the community
development budget for the area is simply closed—which follows the logic
of why the firm embarked on the project in the first instance. Thus projects
are driven by short-term expediency rather than the long-term
development needs of a community. The problem of this short-term
funding is exacerbated by the fact that the major contract managers are
not development specialists. In one extreme case narrated to me by a Shell
manager, SPDC built three town halls in one Niger Delta community as three

community chiefs wanted to benefit personally from contracts from their construction . . .

According to a leaked independent audit of 2001 commissioned by Shell, less than one-third of Shell's development projects were fully successful in the sense that they were functional. The audit found that Shell was still essentially trying to buy off the local people with gifts rather than trying to offer them genuine development; this followed the logic of using CSR to maintain a stable working environment and improve perceptions of Shell. ""

Source: Jedrzej George Frynas, 'The False Developmental Promise of Corporate Social Responsibility: Evidence from Multinational oil Companies', *International Affairs* 81.3 (2005): 581-98.

Frynas goes on to acknowledge some other good work done by Shell and other oil companies and he does not doubt the sincerity of many of the people involved. He also admits that development 'experts' often do no better. But his point is a structural one about playing to one's strengths. He carefully says at the end of his article:

This article does not argue that CSR is discredited because some corporate initiatives have failed. Development agencies and NGOs also have their share of failed development projects, despite their superior developmental expertise . . . The issue is not that firms make mistakes . . . Rather, my argument is that there are fundamental problems about the capacity of private firms to deliver development, and the aspiration of achieving broader development goals through CSR may be flawed.

Frynas's point is essentially directed towards development agencies: do not rely on business to be any good at development and do not follow the fashion of handing over your development responsibilities to multinational companies under the rubric of CSR. But of course there is a lesson here for companies too—an amateurish approach to development activities, unconnected to your real business skills, may buy you short-term support in the local community but will ultimately not convince anyone else.

Frynas argues that the fundamental value of oil companies is not in the peripheral and incompetently implemented activities of building schools and hospitals, but in (shock!) digging up oil. He points out that typically 70–80% of the value of that oil goes to the local government in taxes and the real problem is that government is too corrupt or incompetent to use it for development. If companies really wanted to contribute to development, they'd play more of a role in influencing standards of governance and combating corruption in their operating country to ensure that the 70–80% of value is used properly, rather than using a fraction of their remaining 20–30% to usurp the role of government by building a few token schools. Clearly this is in a company's interest: if you have to pay tax, you might as well try to ensure that it is used in a way that is valued by communities, non-governmental organisations (NGOs) and international agencies. The alternative is to make up for the scepticism about the development value of 'petro-dollars' by paying an additional 'CSR tax' from your profits in order to (often ineffectively) buy off criticism.

⸰⸰ BP development activity around the Tangguh liquid natural gas (LNG) project in West Papua

BP had managed to build some impressive facilities for the villagers. On the first day I walked into New Tanah Merah, music was blaring out of almost every home, a raucous testament to the wonders of free-flow electricity drawn from a new solar-power station. Families sat proudly on their new porches. Small kiosks sold snack foods, cigarettes and soft drinks. With more than 100 identical houses laid out in neat rows, New Tanah Merah looked like a tropical Levittown, the Long Island suburb that set the 20th century standard for suburban replication. BP was eager to show that off. 'Maybe you want to ask about the electricity?' my minder, Jacob Kastanja, interjected during an interview early in my visit. 'It's a big change for them. They have TVs now.' The village also has a Catholic and a Protestant church, a mosque, two schools, a health clinic and new sports fields. There is a new pavilion for the village market and new docks to house what should, if all goes as planned, one day be a fishing fleet composed of new boats promised for each household. Together with New Onar, the result was what BP rightly called a community that could 'probably compete successfully . . . for the title of best physically endowed villages in all of Indonesia'.

That endowment continues to cause problems outside New Tanah Merah. In its recent report, a monitoring panel warned that the BP-built village was fuelling 'jealousy and confusion' among villagers on the opposing north shore of Bintuni Bay. But when I visited, there was also a palpable unease within New Tanah Merah itself. Not about the facilities but about the people themselves: BP people and local people. The company, say its managers privately, is confronting limits to its institutional capacity. It's asking engineers and geophysicists to do social work—which is 'very different from building LNG plants', said one. The locals, too, are confronting a very different world. 'There are a lot of people who are still struggling to adjust,' Thomas Mayera, the chairman of the elected committee which represented Tanah Merah's residents during the resettlement process, told me: 'In the old village we weren't dependent on BP. But here we need time to learn.' ""

Source: Shawn Donnan, *Financial Times*, 26 March 2005.

None of this is to say that you shouldn't be interested in social development issues in the area around your business. In Chapter 5 on security, we discuss how social development can be an important foundation for improved security if it is carried out in a way that undermines rather than reinforces the underlying causes of instability. And in Chapter 6 on partnerships we argue that there are ways of conducting development programmes more effectively by partnering with real experts rather than trying to do it all yourself.

But development experts are right to point out that your development efforts will inevitably be selective and focused in the areas most directly relevant to your business, leaving gaps which need to be filled by something other than the profit motive in the short term. You, in return, can point out that it is your core business rather than the peripheral development activity that is having the real impact and, in time, that effect can and should spread throughout society.

Does CSR make a difference?

The development economist Rhys Jenkins[6] has written about the three ways in which companies might contribute to poverty alleviation:

- Through poor people as customers
- Through poor people as employees and suppliers
- Through developing-country governments as recipients of tax

6 R. Jenkins, 'Globalisation, Corporate Social Responsibility and Poverty', *International Affairs* 81.3 (2005): 525-40.

He believes that these contributions are small (we disagree!) and that CSR does little to increase, and can sometimes reduce, that contribution (we agree!).

Jenkins's first possible mechanism for companies to reduce poverty is the **'distribution channel'**—with poor people as consumers at C.K. Prahalad's famous bottom of the pyramid (see Chapter 1). Jenkins is sceptical.

> Although [Prahalad] provides inspiring examples of success stories in India and other countries, several of the cases which he cites are of not-for-profit organisations and relatively few are foreign investors. He consistently overestimates the potential purchasing power of poor people, often by extending the definition of the poor to include those who are relatively well off by developing-country standards . . . It should also be noted that the fact that some multinational companies (MNCs) sell their products to the poor is no guarantee that they will contribute to either improving the welfare of the poor or reducing poverty . . . The sale of skin lighteners in single-application packets which can be purchased individually by less well-off consumers in Bangladesh is unlikely to contribute to sustainable development.

We think this is a bit harsh and we'll discuss later how seeing poor people as customers *can* have an important effect on poverty. But Jenkins's important question is whether CSR changes any of this. His answer is no—the companies that most implement CSR tend to be those that export consumer goods such as sports gear, garments and toys to rich countries, or extractive industries that export minerals and oil to the West. CSR has little to say about how you treat poor people as customers, perhaps reflecting the fact that it arose as a result of pressure from rich Western consumers and governments rather than the poor in developing countries.

Jenkins's second possible mechanism for businesses to reduce poverty is the **'enterprise channel'**—the role of companies in employing people and buying from local suppliers. He argues that the impact of this will be small because multinationals employ relatively few people in developing countries—19 million in 1998 compared with an estimated worldwide total of 1,200 million people living on less than $1 a day. He further argues that many people employed by MNCs in developing countries are anyway already quite rich and companies rarely reach the poorest people.

We'll discuss later why we think this is a static view that ignores all sorts of spillover effects. But his important point is that CSR initiatives do little to change the arithmetic. There is nothing in CSR that expands the number of people you employ beyond what is already economically optimal and there is nothing that encourages you to employ poorer people. Indeed CSR is likely to make matters worse:

> Indirect negative impacts may also ensue from the efforts of firms to monitor the social impact of their activities. Since it is easier for firms to monitor a small number of large suppliers rather than a myriad of small ones, there is a tendency to concentrate suppliers. However, small and/or informal enterprises are more likely to employ large numbers of poor people, and agricultural smallholders are more likely to be poor than large commercial growers, so such a trend can have a negative effect on the poor. The football stitching industry in Pakistan provides an example: in Sialkot, the shift to concentrate production in factories, in response to concerns about child labour, led to many woman home-workers losing out.

Finally there is the **government revenue channel**. Jenkins again argues that companies are adept at avoiding tax and that CSR has little to say on the subject. He quotes two other academics, Christensen and Murphy, who say:

> It is . . . curious . . . that the debate about CSR, which has touched on virtually every other area of corporate engagement with broader society has scarcely begun to questions companies in the area where their corporate citizenship is most tangible and most important—the payment of tax.

Jenkins acknowledges the emerging CSR debate about transparency, governance and how taxes are *spent*, but laments the lack of emphasis on how companies *avoid* them in the first place.

So, CSR has little to say on the mechanisms by which multinationals could reduce poverty. CSR is not interested in the poor as consumers. Efforts to monitor labour standards can discourage companies from dealing with the very poorest. And companies spend small amounts on highly visible CSR projects while avoiding large amounts of taxes that could help local governments to work properly. Not a very good record.

These warnings about CSR are an important reminder that business cannot and should not become responsible for all aspects of development. There remains an important role for donors, NGOs and governments in tackling the many issues that businesses do not have the capability or incentives to tackle. Business zealots who want to apply the 'business case' and 'business thinking' to all aspects of development are wrong. In the short term, development experts are right to want to defend some of their turf from the encroachments of business.

What business can do for the poor

However, we must not go to the other end of the spectrum. We agree that business, whether or not modified by CSR, cannot meet all development needs. But this does not mean that businesses can do nothing. In particular, while we acknowledge that donors and NGOs are currently important in providing all sorts of services that cannot be justified on a business case, surely the aim of donors and development NGOs must ultimately be to work themselves out of a job. There is no honour in eternally defending a development patch based on some real or imagined development expertise. Instead, the ultimate aim must be to alleviate poverty by handing over to a thriving private sector, strong local communities and a local government providing public services that are sustainably funded by local taxes.

The obvious key to achieving this is economic growth. Growth can come from all sorts of sources—from tapping natural resources to increasing the population or plundering other countries. But the only sustainable way of achieving growth, and particularly growth per capita, is to do more with the capital and labour you've already got by increasing productivity. The economist Marcel Fafchamps says:

> Technological change has long been recognised as an essential ingredient of growth. It is clear to almost everyone that standards of living in developed countries could not have increased the way they have over the last 200 years if it had not been for technological change. There is little doubt that it is the scientific revolution, that is the application of science and technology not only in industry but also in agriculture, medicine and services, that is responsible for the remarkable achievements of the last 200 years. If technological change is the most important engine of growth, economic development then can be seen as a modernisation process, that is as an historical transformation by which an undeveloped economy joins the scientific era.[7]

7 Marcel Fafchamps, 'Engines of Growth and Africa's Economic Performance', July 2000; www.economics.ox.ac.uk/members/marcel.fafchamps/homepage/engines.pdf, 24 May 2006.

> ❝ The founder and chairman of the MIT Media Lab, Nicholas Negroponte, wants to create a $100 portable computer for the developing world . . . The portable PCs will be shipped directly to education ministries, with China first on the list. Only orders of 1 million or more units will be accepted . . . Major companies from Hewlett-Packard to Microsoft to Dupont, facing saturated markets in the richest industrial countries, have shown an interest in developing less expensive products to sell in low-income countries in South Asia, Africa and Latin America. ❞
>
> Source: 'The hundred-buck PC', *Red Herring*, 29 January 2005.

As Fafchamps points out, we should see technology not only as machines and electronics but also as ways of working, management systems and organisational structures.

How then should a developing country acquire these technologies and start to implement them in the economy?

Basic education is clearly essential in creating a critical mass of people who can apply technology to the economy, and this is always likely to be a job for government not business. Educated people could, then, in theory, invent everything from scratch in order to catch up, but why bother when it already exists elsewhere?

Instead it may seem attractive to 'copy' everything from a distance by plundering academic papers, blueprints and management books, but this is notoriously difficult to do. Much modern technology, particularly about ways of working, tends to be 'tacit' knowledge that is not totally captured anywhere on paper or the internet. An organisation that is capable of producing some useful piece of technology is a complex mixture of culture, rules of thumb and organisational structures that may not be completely understood even by the people within it. So, while one way of applying the benefits of computing to an economy would be to study Dell and try to copy it, a faster and more effective way is simply to buy its computers or even better encourage it to set up a factory locally.

We're sorry to labour this as it should be entirely obvious, but it's a point that's often missed by the anti-globalisation lobby. If we want to bring the advantages of technology to developing countries, instead of supplying blueprints and theory, we can supply products, people and organisations which 'embody' the knowledge. We might sniff at consumer goods and, of course, there are examples of products such as skin lighteners that are difficult to justify. But the sale of a computer or a mobile phone brings the benefits of years of technological and managerial experimentation directly to consumers and, in turn, gives them the power to create further value. The fact that the computer may not be sold to the poorest person in the land does not alter the fact that it instantly increases the productive power of the country as a whole. The same is obviously also true of capital goods such as machinery, which local businesses can use to create value.

So what Jenkins calls the 'distribution channel' can have a huge impact on growth because products embody the benefits of new technology. Not all of it will be good or productive, but some of it will be. And if an entrepreneur uses a mobile phone or a lathe to create a business and in turn employs a poor person, it does not matter for poverty alleviation that the phone was not initially sold to the poor person himself.

** The Pew Center for the People and the Press surveyed 38,000 people in 44 nations, with excellent coverage of the developing world in all regions. In general, there is a positive view of growing economic integration worldwide. But what was striking in the survey is that views of globalization are distinctly more positive in low-income countries than in rich ones.

While most people worldwide viewed growing global trade and business ties as good for their country, only 28% of people in the US and Western Europe thought that such integration was 'very good.' In Vietnam and Uganda, in contrast, the figures for 'very good' stood at 56% and 64%, respectively. Although these countries were particularly pro-globalization, developing Asia (37%) and Sub-Saharan Africa (56%) were far more likely to find integration 'very good' than industrialized countries. Conversely, a significant minority (27% of households) in rich countries thought that 'globalization has a bad effect on my country,' compared to negligible numbers of households with that view in developing Asia (9%) or Sub-Saharan Africa (10%) . . .

The anti-globalization movement often claims that integration leads to growing inequality within countries, with no benefits going to the poor. Generally, this is not true. There are certainly some countries in which inequality has risen, like China and the US, but there is no worldwide trend. Most important, in the developing countries that are growing well as a result of integration and other reforms, rapid growth translates into rapid poverty reduction. The total number of extreme poor (living on less than $1 per day measured at purchasing power parity) increased throughout history up to about 1980. Since 1980 that number declined by 200 million, while world population increased by 1.8 billion. The progress is heartening, but there are still 1.2 billion people living in poverty.[**]

Source: David Dollar, Director of Development Policy, World Bank, 'The Poor Like Globalization', YaleGlobal, 23 June 2003 (available at http://yaleglobal.yale.edu/display.article?id=1934).

The second key contribution of business is through the 'employment channel'—the effects that multinational companies have by employing people or using them as suppliers. Some of the largest such poverty-reducing backward linkages are in the agri-business sector. Nestlé, for example, has something like 10,000 agricultural extension officers worldwide whose sole purpose is to build the constancy and quality of supply of agricultural products (much of it coffee) into Nestlé factories. This backward linkage induces extraordinary levels of poverty reduction, especially in poor rural areas.

The amazing thing is the impact is currently not measured. We don't really know how large the impact really is. But we do know that an MNC can indeed have large impacts on poverty when it decides on backward linkage options. For example, Pepsico recently opened a state-of-the-art potato chip factory in the Indian state of West Bengal. Wherever it had opened, the factory would have had a need for potatoes. But by opening in a relatively poor state, the Pepsico factory reduced more poverty through its contract farming arrangements than it would have through sourcing potatoes in a richer Indian state.

However, the point is not simply about the wages that are being paid and whether or not they go to the poorest in society. The important contribution is that companies are transferring a complex body of knowledge to their employees and suppliers, not only in formal training sessions or 'technology transfer' agreements but also in day-to-day sharing of experience on how to provide valuable goods and services. *Employees* become more productive because they are working in an institution that can provide the equipment and management practices that are needed to fully utilise their efforts. This is a valuable end in itself but, over time, these employees may also use their learned skills to set up their own enterprises or to form an attractive pool of talent to attract further investment. Similarly, *suppliers* have the incentives and the advice they need to improve their own capabilities. Again, this is both an end in itself and also a contribution to creating an ecosystem of competent suppliers to support existing local and international businesses, and to attract further foreign investors into the country.

If this sounds a bit utopian, fortunately there's emerging evidence that supports this view. As foreshadowed in Chapter 1, studies have shown that local companies that directly supply multinationals become more productive. Emphasising the fact that the knowledge that is being transferred is tacit and passed on through direct co-operation, one cannot find an effect on companies in the vicinity of a multinational if they don't have a direct relationship. Copying at arm's length doesn't work—technology is passed on by personal contact.

The main engines of transmission of technology are transnational corporations.

Source: Professor Sanjaya Lall, *Competitiveness, Skills and Technology* (Cheltenham, UK: Edward Elgar, 2001).

Contributing to a country's economic infrastructure

The final key way in which business can support economic growth is by contributing to an economic infrastructure of regulation, laws and economic policy-making (the knowledge of how to govern a free-market economy), which benefits existing businesses in the country, both local and foreign, and serves to stimulate further internal and foreign investment. Paying taxes is an important element of contributing to governance, but so is knowledge transfer. Once again we see that, contrary to Rhys Jenkins's comments, you cannot measure a company's impact solely by counting the number of poor people it directly sells to or employs or by the taxes it pays, but instead you have to look at the entire impact it has on the overall economic and governance environment.

Your host country is not a passive recipient of investment and aid. Most countries will be working hard to create an attractive business environment and trying to attract the investors that they feel will create the most economic advantage and transfer the most know-how. If you can understand their reform priorities and how they are trying to compete with other countries for investment, you will be able to present your business in the most attractive light and secure the most support for your activities. Your complaints and concerns can be presented not as self-interested whingeing, but instead as an attempt to help the country understand how to attract and retain international investment.

You will find that countries are increasingly trying to compete on the *detail* of micro-economic policy and regulation. They should welcome your help in solving the problems and in creating a business ecosystem that will encourage further investment. As currency crises and huge budget deficits become largely a thing of the past, attention is turning to the practicalities of doing business.

The battle for macro-economic stability in developing countries has largely been won. The world knows so much more now about its macro-economic levers—and is so much better at setting them—that large economic shocks are becoming fewer and farther between. And the shocks that do occur are being better managed. This achievement is especially significant given how much more money circulates around the world these days and so speedily. Hyper-inflation is a thing of the past. We no longer suffer economic depressions brought on by economic policy missteps.

The roles and influences of central banks on monetary policy and inflation are much better understood. The theory and practice of exchange rates are also better understood, especially the consequences of adopting one type of exchange rate regime over another. Consequently, current account positions tend to self-manage a little more than they used to. Thus, for MNCs investing in developing countries, the issue of macro-economic factors is becoming less important.

On the other hand, businesses are now looking much more at comparative micro-economic issues in host economies.

- How long does it take to clear customs?
- What is their duty system like and do they have a customs duty drawback system?
- What is the price of corruption as a percentage of overall cost structure?
- How difficult is it to obtain and retain an electricity connection?
- Are work permits readily available for expatriates?
- Does it take a day or a year to repatriate profit dividends?
- How much above the Organisation for Economic Co-operation and Development (OECD) average is the annual insurance premium for expatriate managers and their families?

In practice, these questions—and the certainty of the answers—are the most critical factors for MNCs in developing countries these days.

Of course, sometimes host economies can still suffer at the hands of the vagaries of international economic policy changes. For example, with the ending of the global Multi-Fibre Arrangement (MFA) at the end of 2004, massive structural changes have occurred in the garment and apparel manufacturing sector around the world. Although it is not yet completely apparent, this will ensure a drift in investment for garment manufacturing away from places such as Cambodia, Fiji, Bangladesh and Vietnam to, for example, China and, to a lesser extent, Mexico.

In the face of such changes, investors are looking at developing countries to exhibit competitiveness in other areas. Chief among them is standards and compliance. Whereas, before, investors could rely on such incentives as MFA quotas, they now are looking for other competitive advantages. For example, if a host-country government cannot provide a good framework for phytosanitary regulations, it will not succeed in attracting investment in the food and beverage sector. So for developing countries as they race to attract and retain investment, attention to the smaller micro-economic issues is now the order of the day. And, for MNCs, this represents a great opportunity to advise on these issues in a way that contributes to stronger business fundamentals.

Do these contributions to growth help the poor?

There can be little doubt that the presence of multinational companies causes economic growth through technology transfer, increased productivity and better micro-economic management. But what if all the benefits are stripped by the multinationals themselves or by already rich locals? That would defeat most of the argument if we are interested in poverty alleviation rather than overall economic performance. Fortunately, there's evidence on this too. A famous World Bank paper, *Growth is Good for the Poor*, looked at a range of developing countries and compared their growth figures against the change in poor people's incomes. The study showed that, on average across all countries, the benefit of growth for the poor is 1:1—the poor gain proportionately as much as everyone else from improved economic performance. The paper has attracted some criticism for not looking beyond the averages to the experience of individual countries, but no one has disproved the basic conclusion and certainly no one has proved that growth is *bad* for the poor.

The best summary of current knowledge, and a signpost to this book's argument, is probably from Professor Stefan Dercon:

> Some have argued in recent years that the best possible policy for the poor is simply to stimulate growth. 'Growth is good for the poor' became more than a title of an often quoted paper: for some it is a Credo. The essential point of this research . . . was that on average across the sample of the world, a one percent increase in mean income in a country also resulted in a one percent increase in the mean income of the 20 percent poorest in society. Even if one may question elements of the method used, this fact is hard to dispute. The main qualification is related to the interpretation of this result. By virtue of its method, it picks up the average effect, meaning that in many countries the impact on the poor is even more positive, but in others the impact on the poor is much smaller. The main lesson is that in some countries growth is achieved that is largely in favour of the poor; in others growth is much less so in their favour. The challenge is therefore to identify growth policies that benefit the poor most.[8]

This book is about the business contribution to poverty alleviation rather than to economic development because we specifically want to examine how companies might benefit from and contribute to 'pro-poor' growth. The link between profits and growth is obvious—growth is just a measure of the increase in economic activity and, if your profits increase in a country, then clearly that contributes directly to the growth figure, regardless of how the profits are produced. Telling companies to improve their profits by seeking to improve economic growth is a tautology. But we'll argue that specifically seeking *pro-poor* growth can provide clues to overcoming some of the inefficiencies of operating in a developing country, strengthening your long-term strategic position and protecting your reputation.

---

8 S. Dercon, *Poverty Traps and Development: The Equity–Efficiency Trade-Off Revisited* (paper prepared for the Conference on Growth, Inequality and Poverty, organised by the Agence française de développement and the European Development Research Network [EUDN], September 2003; www.economics.ox.ac.uk/members/stefan.dercon/poverty%20traps.pdf, 8 March 2006).

The global poverty trap

Jeffrey Sachs, economist, recently claimed that due to the realpolitik of the aid business, the US untied development assistance in 2003 (the type that excludes that spent on American non-Governmental organisations, consultants and contractors) amounted to just 18 cents for each of the 650m people living in low-income sub-Saharan Africa.

So even if we combine this 18 cents per capita contribution with what is available from others, we are not going to get much more than $1 per person per year in sub-Saharan Africa. Multiply that by 10 or even 100 for new aid pledges currently being sought, and it is still only $100 per poor African per year. Clearly, much more than aid is needed.

Source: Kurt Hoffman, Director of the Shell Foundation, 'Lack of Investment is the Tragedy in Africa', *Financial Times*, 10 June 2005; available at www.shellfoundation.org/index.php?articleID=36.

Development advocates are right to point out that businesses cannot do everything in development and that CSR will do little to change that fact. But, if we agree that the only sustainable source of growth and poverty alleviation is the application of technology to goods and services, it is difficult to see what significant progress can be made *without* business. Aid flows are small and show no signs of increasing to the point where they could directly fund a better life for each of the world's poor. Aid can fill some of the gaps left by business and can contribute to an attractive business environment, but ultimately only business can create the new value that's required to bring the world up to a decent standard of living.

In contrast to the views of the anti-business and anti-globalisation lobby, the real gap in development is in those countries where international business is not yet willing to go. As we've identified, companies tend to be drawn to places where other businesses are already operating, for the good reason that this will guarantee an infrastructure of suppliers, services, intermediaries and customers. We can see this operating within a country as well as in the world as a whole—businesses are not spread out evenly across a country but are concentrated in a few cities because they want to be close to other businesses. Over time the cities become congested with high labour and property prices, which for some companies outweigh the benefits of the city. Companies then move but they do not spread out evenly; they form another cluster somewhere else in another city or business zone.

Thus to understand under-development, we have to look at a country systematically rather than focus on one region at a time and wonder why it is under-developed; one can understand why Cornwall has little business activity only if we understand the attraction to business of operating in the nearby cities of Exeter or Bristol instead. We can see that there is a sort of poverty trap operating here for regions and countries. Once a location has, for whatever reason, become a business cluster, it is very hard for another nearby location to start from zero and catch up.

If you disagree, imagine trying to create an industry in your nearest small village that consistently produces blockbuster films on the same scale as Hollywood. How would you instantly put in place a complex network of artists, agents, financiers, producers, publicists and call girls to attract the major studios? Of course, Hollywood didn't have always have a film industry, but for complex reasons of climate, culture and luck it was able to establish one just as the industry was starting out. Eighty years later, it would be difficult to start from scratch and win.

On a global scale, we can see this happening with China and India at the moment. Companies that have begun to find the US and Western Europe too expensive are moving to China and India because they have an emerging infrastructure of high-quality service providers and an increasingly experienced workforce. This process has been helped by the advent of new technologies such as electronics, which have high value compared with their size and weight, and can thus be economically shipped long distances to the main markets in the West. China and India have benefited hugely from opening up to international trade and investment at the same time as the emergence of a technology that was ready to move to a distant location.

So China and India have specialised in a growth technology and are not yet 'full up'—they can still attract a lot more foreign companies before labour or property prices begin to match those in the West. As long as this situation lasts, it is difficult to see why a company would prefer to operate in another country with similar business costs but less business infrastructure. In time, of course, China and India will become congested and a new cluster will form elsewhere, but it may take a long time before this development domino effect reaches Sierra Leone or the Congo.

This systemic way of looking at the world is problematic for people who believe that business can solve all development problems because it emphasises that globalisation is not going to spread the benefits of business evenly around the world. No matter how much we may want business to be active in the poorest countries, it may not always be realistic in the medium term, as businesses follow each other to more attractive destinations.

But perhaps this does at least make the proper division of labour between business and development much clearer. Companies will achieve rapid poverty reduction in the countries that are lucky enough to form new business clusters in the global economic system. This will allow development professionals to focus their limited resources on the leftover unlucky countries, locked in a global poverty trap, who can't attract business because they haven't already attracted business. Their aim in these leftover countries must be to find ways to overcome the poverty trap to attract some initial business and, in the meantime, alleviate the symptoms of poverty through philanthropic activities. As we have seen, CSR is unlikely to contribute effectively to any of this and may even discourage companies from investing in the poorest countries where it is most difficult to monitor and maintain standards.

> " Most companies have stuck to the strategies they've traditionally deployed, which emphasize standardized approaches to new markets while sometimes experimenting with a few local twists. As a result, many multinational corporations are struggling to develop successful strategies in emerging markets.
>
> Part of the problem, we believe, is that the absence of specialized intermediaries, regulatory systems, and contract-enforcing mechanisms hampers the implementation of globalization strategies. Companies in developed countries usually take for granted the critical role that 'soft' infrastructure plays in the execution of their business models in their home markets. But that infrastructure is often underdeveloped or absent in emerging markets. "
>
> Source: Tarun Khanna, Krishna Palepu and Jayant Sinha, 'Strategies that Fit Emerging Markets', *Harvard Business Review*, June 2005.

This completes the final piece of our argument about the links between businesses and poverty reduction. Most of our recommendations are about how a company, once they are in a country, can operate more effectively by adopting a 'poverty perspective'. But companies that are confident about operating in difficult environments and skilled at filling gaps in local infrastructure can also be more adventurous about where they choose to invest in the first place. Companies can benefit from lower costs and welcoming governments if they don't follow the pack to China and India, but choose somewhere that desperately needs some initial investors in order to enter the global system. Companies can make a convincing development case for their presence, not only because of the value they create by their operations, but because they are helping to overcome that country's poverty trap by contributing to the formation of a local business infrastructure and thereby attracting further foreign investors.

But where are the incentives?

This book is making the business case for reducing poverty in poor countries. We will argue that there are numerous advantages in thinking about poverty: you will be a better manager and your company will achieve higher profits at lower risk, if you include a poverty perspective in your day-to-day decision-making.

And, from the economic development point of view, what matters is not the mere presence of a company in a country but the way in which day-to-day business decisions are made. It is strongly in the interests of development people to influence not only the macro-decisions about whether to enter a country, but also the micro-decisions about how companies behave once they get there.

So we believe there are already many benefits to both companies and development people in thinking about the links between business and poverty. But we also acknowledge that the advantages for business in doing something about poverty are not always obvious and often require short-term cost and risk in return for long-term, sometimes intangible, benefit. If that weren't the case, it would all be so self-evident and easy that everybody would be doing it already.

So, in addition to all the incremental and subtle benefits that we try to identify in this book, we might also ask what are the specific formal incentives for companies to start thinking in this way? How could development agencies, governments and NGOs prompt companies to do more on poverty and, in particular, help companies to overcome the difficulties of constructing a viable business case for poverty alleviation when the costs are immediate and incurred solely by the company and the benefits are distant and shared between the company and the poor? How can people who are interested in development tip the balance and turn what may be a marginal business case into a clear and immediate priority for companies?

There is already no shortage of incentives and factors that multinational corporations need to consider when making the general business decision of whether to make a new or expanded investment in a developing country. Just to name a few, the list includes:

- Profitability and return on capital
- Access to new markets
- Levels of political risk
- Access to appropriately skilled and priced labour and other factors of production
- Integration into other aspects of their global businesses
- Supply chain efficiencies
- Governance standards and corruption levels in the host economy
- Preferential trade arrangements
- Political risk insurance from their home-country governments or international agencies
- Tax holidays
- Investment subsidies
- Access to local capital and financial markets
- The costs of doing business such as licensing and customs delays
- Labour standards
- Labour productivity
- Local corporate social responsibility frameworks and potential effects on global brand and reputation
- The existence of an applicable investment treaty between the home and host economies

This is quite an overwhelming list. When going through the even longer version of this list, the absence of any incentive whatsoever relating to the reduction of poverty becomes apparent. To be precise, our review has not found a single formalised mechanism or incentive available to the world's private multinational corporations (the repository of most of the world's capital, technology and resources) to encourage them to reduce poverty in developing countries through direct investment.

Of course, if a multinational company does reduce poverty as a result of their normal business investments and activities, that's great, and we argue that this happens all the time—even if it is just a happy side-effect and there is no one actually counting the impact the business is having on poverty. And if, in the odd event that a multinational corporation doesn't achieve a reduction in poverty as a result of its investment, well, that is not surprising given that there were no incentives to do so in the first place.

Yet this absence of incentive relating to poverty reduction contrasts starkly with the growing international consensus of the pre-eminence of the goal of poverty reduction in the world's poor countries, and with the level of financial and rhetorical commitment to that goal made by the world's governments and government-funded development agencies. The absence of such an incentive becomes even more obvious when remembering that the net resources of the world's multinational corporations that can be invested in developing countries dwarfs those that are at the disposal of development organisations. In fact, as we have argued, business in poor countries reduces poverty more than any other known means.

We're only telling you this because we think you could do something about it. There are already some straws in the wind that indicate that international organisations are beginning to think about the problem of incentives. Harvard Business School Professor George Lodge wrote an influential article[9] which argued that development funds should be used to incentivise major companies to carry out infrastructure development projects through the vehicle of a 'World Development Corporation'—a sort of private-sector analogue to the World Bank. The United Nations Development Programme (UNDP) Commission on the Private Sector and Development acknowledged the need for donors to work more effectively with the private sector, though it stopped short of making specific recommendations on incentives for multinational companies. We discuss the problems of incentives and multinational support, including some false starts, in more detail in Chapter 6 on forming partnerships.

So, if as you're reading this book you think 'nice idea but it wouldn't work', pause to think about what the obstacles are and what you'd need to tip the balance. Write your thoughts down and let donors know (we give details for the UNDP Commission below). The door is wide open for companies to influence development policy in their own interest and in the interests of the poor.

---

9 G.C. Lodge, 'The Corporate Key: Using Big Business to Fight Global Poverty', *Foreign Affairs*, 81.4 (2002): 13ff.

Follow-up questions

How does your business assist a country 'to enter the scientific era' through the people you employ, the products you sell and the taxes you pay?

What do you know about running a business and producing valuable products? How much of that knowledge is being transferred to the local economy?

Do your CSR efforts add or subtract from the above?

Do you know enough about development to confidently manage your CSR projects?

How could you further your own interests, while contributing to development, by helping the host government and donors to develop better policies, laws and regulations?

Further reading

The UNDP's Commission on the Private Sector and Development published a report, *Unleashing Entrepreneurship: Making Business Work for the Poor*, in March 2004 that outlines why the private sector is important to development and what role multinational companies can play. As of March 2006, it was available for free download at the Commission's website (www.undp.org/cpsd).

The Wealth and Poverty of Nations: Why Some Are So Rich and Some Are So Poor by David Landes (published in hardback in New York by Little, Brown & Company in 1998 and in paperback in London by Abacus in 1999) and *Guns, Germs and Steel: The Fates of Human Societies* by Jared Diamond (revised edition published in New York by W.W. Norton in 2005) both examine the fundamentals of why some societies are richer than others. Landes focuses on the cultural and political conditions that support technological advance, while Diamond looks at how innovations spread. Both are masterpieces.

For links to these resources and other relevant material, go to www.makepovertybusiness.com.

What is poverty?
How many people are poor?

Turning up in a developing country

As a multinational corporation manager, have you ever put yourself in the position of the multiple civil servants and government agencies with whom you will be dealing upon arrival in the host developing country? It is a useful exercise. They are often incredibly poor, surrounded by (and involved in) corruption, operating in a severely dysfunctional bureaucracy, and with very low levels of autonomy (we have been to places where the government minister allocated the car parking spaces because no one below him was willing or able to make the decision). More often than not (and certainly at the more senior levels), they will be well-intentioned and capable people, simply captured by the structures within which they find themselves. Some of them will have a sense of perspective of their own situation and some will have no other reference points.

Imagine you work in the local investment promotion office and you are approached by a would-be investor wanting to set up, for example, a wastewater treatment company. You lack resources, industry knowledge, authority, and the pertinent laws are fuzzy, archaic or non-existent. You are mindful of the agenda of your government minister. There is no formalised incentive structure in your office. Accordingly, your response will be one of self-preservation and self-interest. This probably means prevarication, denial, avoidance of risk and lack of interest in the technicalities. As a potential investor from a rich, technically advanced and value-adding multinational corporation, you are probably stunned at the inert response. You were expecting to be swallowed up in a sea of gratitude—after all, you are bringing in new capital and technology, and promising to create new jobs.

But the truth is you still have much work to do to obtain appropriate government approvals and guarantees. A good place to start is by identifying a common vocabulary with your hosts and aligning your respective incentives, particularly around tangible opportunities for poverty reduction.

The good news is that those parts of developing-country governments responsible for attracting and retaining your FDI are becoming increasingly sensitised to the importance of increased private investment—and thus reduced poverty—in their countries. Notably, most developing countries now have Poverty Reduction Strategy Papers (PRSPs) and they are normally, although not always, produced with the input of those civil servants responsible for implementing the strategy and achieving the objectives. These strategies invariably place the growth of private investment, including FDI, at their centre (along with other things such as access to primary healthcare, greater availability of credit to micro-entrepreneurs and small businesses, and better primary education). But, equally invariably, there is no direct and quantifiable link between the conceptual task of growing private investment and the tangible requirement of reducing poverty. People know that there's a link in theory, but may struggle to see how your specific investment proposal will help. It is your job to make the connection clear.

The growing importance to developing-country governments of poverty reduction thus becomes a useful fulcrum that potential private investors and MNC managers need to take advantage of. A two-page description of a potential investment that includes the vocabulary of poverty reduction will be well received by a host developing-country government. Of course, a new investor always needs to know about tax rates, double taxation agreements, labour costs and labour laws, and the legal framework for profit repatriation. But, these days, they also need to know about the government's poverty reduction strategy. An investment proposal that conforms with, and contributes to, that strategy will be much better received.

The language and measurement of poverty

We could construct an entire academic career and secure millions of pounds' worth of grants if we chose to go into the technicalities of measuring global poverty. But we're not going to do that. Instead we're going to give a quick outline of the economists' 'best guess' at how many people have an extremely low income and then we'll discuss wider definitions of poverty that do not look at income alone. Our purpose is to outline what problem you are trying to solve when you try to reduce poverty and to emphasise that reducing poverty is not simply a question of giving people more money. If your company chooses to emphasise its contribution to poverty reduction, this chapter will also discuss how to present your activities in a way that is most relevant to governments, opinion-formers and development agencies.

The standard definition of extreme poverty is people who live on the equivalent of less than 1 US dollar a day. This measure has been bandied around so much that it is easy to forget just how desperate such a living standard would be. The most important thing to remember is that the measurement is adjusted for living costs in the relevant country. This is calculated by:

- Working out what a person who earned $1 a day in the USA could buy (clearly not much)
- Working out how much that level of consumption would cost in the country under study
- Counting how many people earn less than that

This is the purchasing power parity (PPP) method, made famous by *The Economist*'s well-known 'Big Mac' index, which relates economic data to the cost of a burger in different countries. You can find PPP exchange rates in most economic data sources next to the currency exchange rates.

So we are not measuring people who actually earn $1 a day converted at international exchange rates (this might allow a relatively comfortable lifestyle because prices in many developing countries are low). We are measuring how many people can consume the same as a person who earned $1 per day in the USA (very few such people actually exist in the USA). To put it into further perspective, cows in the European Union receive a subsidy of $2 a day and, by 2015, it is expected that only 0.3% of people in Europe and Central Asia would live on the equivalent of $1 a day. So the poor people that you see in inner cities in Europe or America are simply not that poor by the definition we are using.

In 2005, the number of people in developing countries estimated to be living on the equivalent of less than $1 a day was 1.1 billion. This compares with a total population in developing countries of 5 billion and a global population of 6 billion. Around 300 million of these people live in Africa and 400 million in South Asia, with the remainder mostly living in East Asia and the Pacific.

Among all these bleak figures, it is easy to forget that huge progress is being made. One of the UN's Millennium Development Goals[10] was to halve, between 1990 and 2015, the proportion of people who lived on less than $1 a day. This sounds preposterously ambitious and, for those people who work in development and see it on bland posters every day, it has become a bit boring. But the astonishing news is that it is very likely to be achieved. Between 1990 and 2005, the proportion of people in developing countries living under the $1 poverty line fell from 28% to 21% and is projected to fall to 10% by 2015, thus more than achieving the Millennium Development Goal. In absolute terms, the reduction in the number of poor people is from 1.5 billion in 1981 to 0.6 billion in 2015. To put this sort of extraordinary progress into more human terms, my grandmother's life expectancy when she was born in the UK in 1900 was lower than the average life expectancy for low-income countries today.

We mostly have China to thank for this excellent progress. In 1981, China was among the poorest countries, with more than 60% of its population living on less than $1 a day. China's poverty rate was halved by 1990 and halved again by 2001. By 2015, East Asia and the Pacific are expected to contain only 3% of the world's poor compared with 53% in 1981. The fact that this has mostly been achieved by Chinese and international business people taking advantage of an increasingly open economy, rather than by people consciously seeking to reach the Millennium Development Goals, should give critics of globalisation pause for thought. India is beginning to contribute to the reduction too; it currently has more poor people than China despite having a smaller population, but, as it too opens up to international investment, the number of very poor people in South Asia is expected to halve from 431 million in 2001 to 216 million in 2015.

The exception to all this good news is, of course, Africa. The absolute number of very poor people in Africa is expected to rise from 227 million in 1990 to 340 million in 2015—the only reason that the *proportion* of Africans who are poor will not also increase is because of fast population growth. As

10   See www.un.org/millenniumgoals (accessed 20 March 2006).

the large countries of Asia make significant progress and Africa declines, Africa's share of the world's poor will increase from 11% in 1981 to 57% in 2015. Africa is the only region that is *not* on target to reach the Millennium poverty target and 38% of Africans are expected to live on less than $1 a day by 2015, down only slightly from 44% in 1990.

Criticism of the $1 a day measure

Not everyone is happy with the $1 a day measure and there is some suspicion that it has been chosen because it is a media-friendly and catchy round number, rather than because it relates to any fundamental assessment of human needs. It is certainly true to say that it captures only those people who are poor by the standards of poor countries and extremely, desperately poor by Western standards. It sets the bar much lower than the level we would consider a reasonable poverty line in the West and, as a result, some economists have argued that it underestimates the extent of global poverty. It is easy to forget when we look at the optimistic projections that the people lifted above the $1 a day line have not been propelled into a life of ease and luxury. The number of people living on between $1 and $2 a day increased from 2.4 billion in 1981 to 2.7 billion in 2001, as people previously under $1 a day joined the group. Imagine living on less than $700 *per year* in the USA and you will realise that these people are still very poor by any reasonable measure.

There are also numerous technical objections to the measure based on the lack of reliable data in many parts of the world and the difficulty of properly comparing the poor's cost of living in different countries. But for our purposes the measures will probably do. What we are looking for is an idea of trends over time and rough comparisons across countries and regions rather than absolute figures. Most importantly from the business perspective, we are aiming for an idea of how to present poverty reduction figures in a way that is meaningful to governments and development agencies. There is no doubt that the $1 a day measure has become the most popular method of communicating international progress on poverty alleviation.

Estimating the value of business to poverty reduction

It would be nice if you could just take the size of your investment in a country and use a simple formula to convert that into a figure for poverty reduction. Unfortunately, there is no existing set of estimates that helps to calculate how much poverty will be reduced, on average, in any given developing country through an extra dollar of private investment. This might be slightly surprising, but reflects the sad fact that until recently there has not been much consensus in development circles on whether foreign investment has any positive impact at all.

But, as we indicate throughout the book, the effects of foreign investment depend very much on the nature of the investment, the extent of technology transfer and the number of linkages to local companies. So, even if we did have an average effect of all types of foreign investment in all countries, it might not be very meaningful—particularly given the difficulty of finding reliable data across a wide range of countries. Additionally, the maths gets hard because it is difficult to separate out cause and effect; foreign direct investment causes economic growth, but economic growth also attracts further foreign investment. There may also be hidden causes that affect both growth and investment—for example, a change of laws and regulations may contribute simultaneously to increased local economic activity and greater foreign investment. All of this means that studies have to be done with extreme care and can easily be challenged by people who want to reach a different conclusion that better fits their political views or preconceptions.

So starting from the top down and looking for a simple formula to turn the size of your investment into a poverty reduction figure is going to be very difficult to do for most companies, particularly as development economists are still not agreed on exactly what the relationships are between growth, investment and poverty reduction. We should also note that development agencies cannot currently make analogous calculations on the effect a dollar of their aid money has on growth and poverty reduction; in 2000 a World Bank report said: 'despite the billions of dollars spent on development assistance each year, there is still very little known about the actual impact of projects on the poor'.[11] So the lack of clarity in companies is unsurprising.

---

11   J. Baker, *Evaluating the Impact of Development Projects on Poverty: A Handbook for Practitioners—Directions in Development* (Washington, DC: World Bank, 2000).

We may, however, have better luck if we take a bottom–up approach and not try to achieve a generic global theory. We could simply count the people working for our company and for direct suppliers who have been lifted out of poverty by doing business with us. As things stand, even the biggest MNCs don't (and aren't able to) represent what they do in these terms. The average MNC operating in a developing country, when speaking of its operations, can normally tell you its profit and loss position, the state of its balance sheet, the number of employees on the payroll, and the amount of taxes it is paying. But it has no systems to record the number of people, within a given footprint, that its operations have lifted out of extreme or moderate poverty.

Given that poverty reduction is the predominant global political objective of the times, not least due to poverty's role as a crucible for terrorism and instability, there is a strong case for business to anchor more firmly what it does in terms of effects on poverty. For example, a natural resource extraction business, about to begin to operate within a defined footprint, will be able as part of its normal cost–benefit analysis work to calculate the overall number of people that will be lifted out of poverty. This is simply a case of taking projections for employment levels within the company and its direct suppliers, and examining which of those employees would currently be defined as poor. Alternatively, a long-standing agriculture company operating in, say, Brazil, and armed with existing official data on poverty levels within its own footprint of operation should be able to calculate the effect it has had on reducing the number of people in poverty by comparing its region of operations with neighbouring regions that have no agro-industry. Thus there are a range of forward-looking predictions and backward-looking impact assessments that could begin to get a measure of the effect that a specific company has had in a specific area.

It is wise to present these figures in a couple of different ways. The $1 a day and $2 a day thresholds are primarily used by the World Bank, other donor agencies and politicians to make high-level policy across a range of countries and to make international comparisons. They can thus be useful for the company chairman to deploy when visiting Washington or if you want to examine a multinational company's total effect on poverty across several countries. However, when development agencies and governments are making plans for a specific country, they tend not to use the generic dollar measures because there is no point in introducing all the uncertainty of international cost-of-living comparisons that come from the purchasing power parity method. Instead you just work in the local currency and with the host government's own definition of the poverty line. Thus, to impress your host government and local development people, you should express your activities in terms of their measures and by how these have contributed to your host country's specific poverty alleviation and development targets.

Poverty Reduction Strategy Papers are the best initial source for understanding host-country and donor priorities. They are prepared by the host government in consultation with a wide range of interested parties and with the support of the International Monetary Fund (IMF) and the World Bank. They're available on the World Bank and IMF websites and are an excellent way of understanding the specifics of poverty alleviation in your host country. It is certainly cheaper and will win you more brownie points to rely on these than to try to do your own research and invent your own priorities for how you think the country should develop.

Of course, the approach of counting only the number of people you have directly lifted out of poverty will significantly underestimate your economic impact. It will miss out the spillover effects we discuss in much of the rest of the book—for example, your impact on the productivity of your suppliers or the extent to which your presence encourages other international companies to invest. But, given the current state of economic knowledge, these gaps are perhaps inevitable. Even if you measure only the direct effect of your operations on poverty, you'll still be doing better than most multinational companies and donor agencies.

A wider definition of poverty

I do not view capitalism as a credo. Much more important to me are freedom, compassion for the poor, respect for the social contract, and equal opportunity. But for the moment, to achieve those goals, capitalism is the only game in town.

Source: Hernando de Soto, *The Mystery of Capital: Why Capitalism Triumphs in the West and Fails Everywhere Else* (New York: Basic Books, 2000).

We've so far taken poverty to be synonymous with low income and this reflects the approach of many development economists. But there is an emerging school of thought that sees the purpose of development to be much more than only increasing economic indicators. This is an important argument because it allows us to capture the much deeper contributions that companies, and the free-market system as a whole, can make to human welfare.

In his book *Development as Freedom*,[12] the Nobel Prize-winning economist Amartya Sen argues that measuring only someone's level of income or consumption gives a very poor estimate of their well-being. He points out that slaves in the American south had consumption levels at least as high as free agricultural labourers. Their life expectancies were similar to the average in France and the Netherlands at the time and higher than that of free urban industrial workers in the USA. But you could hardly say that slaves lived a good life. Indeed, after the abolition of slavery, many planters tried to replicate the old gang system and working practices while replacing the use of force with the incentive of high wages but were unable to attract many workers. Even Karl Marx acknowledged that the capitalist system of free labour was an improvement on pre-capitalist systems of slavery and feudalism.

Sen argues that what matters most to people is not income or consumption but 'the freedom to achieve what they value'. If this sounds a bit abstract, then we can see immediately that it has some important concrete implications—saying that two people have the same income is meaningless as a measure of their ability to live a good life if one is severely disabled and one is healthy; if one has access to free schooling and healthcare and the other doesn't; or if one lives in a dangerous society and the other doesn't. Sen gives the alarming example that, on average, African–American people are significantly richer than people in developing countries but have a lower chance of reaching a mature age than people in China, Sri Lanka or much of India.

Sen does not argue that income is unimportant—it is often a means to achieve other aspects of well-being. But it is not the whole story. Other aspects of freedom—including the freedom to make one's own choices free of unreasonable constraint from governments, oppressive communities, criminals or soldiers, and the freedom to work and trade with whomever you choose—are also important in their own right. In particular, Sen says that we might choose a free market even if we did not believe it was the most efficient way of producing economic growth:

> to be generically against markets would be almost as odd as being
> generically against conversations between people (even though

12 Published by Oxford University Press in 1999.

some conversations are clearly foul and cause problems for others—or even for the conversationalists themselves). The freedom to exchange words, or goods, or gifts does not need defensive justification in terms of their favourable but distant effects; they are part of the way human beings in society live and interact with each other (unless stopped by regulation or fiat). The contribution of the market mechanism to economic growth is, of course, important, but this comes only after the direct significance of the freedom to interchange—words, goods, gifts—has been acknowledged.

This argument is important because it is sometimes argued that a 'benevolent dictatorship', such as existed in Singapore, is better at producing economic growth than a democracy. There is emerging evidence that this is wrong in practice—well-governed free societies tend to grow much quicker than autocracies. But Sen's point is that there is a more fundamental theoretical misunderstanding at work; if your aim is increasing freedom for its own sake rather than just income then, by definition, you cannot achieve that by increasing autocracy.

Sen is no mad libertarian and he emphasises that there is a proper role for legitimate government in regulation, rule of law and the provision of public services such as health and education which will contribute directly to people's freedom. For example, when we examine the positive effect that economic growth has on life expectancy (or freedom from premature death), we see that one of the most important elements is not growth per se but the effect it has on government spending on health.

The nice element of all this is that the different aspects of freedom, though each important in their own right, also tend to mutually reinforce each other. Freedom from ill-health contributes to people's ability to earn a decent wage and vice versa. Spending on education increases people's life choices, but also has an impressive impact on economic growth. And, as touched upon above, greater political freedom tends to produce better economic results.

The United Nations Development Programme has tried to capture the work of people like Sen by compiling a Human Development Index, which combines measures of per capita income with statistics for life expectancy, schooling and literacy. Of course, the different weight you choose to give to these different measures in order to compile an aggregate score is highly subjective and somewhat political—perhaps only development people and international bureaucrats would argue that Belgium (ranked 6) is a better place to live than Italy (ranked 21). But we might all agree that Norway and Sweden (the top two) are better places to live than Niger and Sierra Leone (the bottom two) and that our reasons for saying so are not only because they have a higher per capita income.

How does business contribute to 'development as freedom'?

> " I regard the extension of the range of choice, that is, an increase in the range of effective alternatives open to the people, as the principal objective and criterion of economic development; and I judge a measure principally by its probable effects on the range of alternatives open to individuals. "
>
> Source: Peter Bauer, *Dissent on Development: Studies and Debates in Development Economics* (London: Weidenfeld & Nicolson, 1971).

When we lived in Indonesia, we both spent time at a language school run by an Indonesian family. The elderly father of the house had spent most of his adult years working in the closed economy of President Sukarno, when the only jobs available for well-educated people had been in the civil service or the military. The result was that he had been highly constrained in his behaviour and life choices; if you didn't conform to social, religious and political norms, you just couldn't get a job.

His children had a much wider range of choices open to them. The daughter ran the language school and a travel business on the side. The younger son was considering a career in architecture or banking, perhaps with one of the international banks that were beginning to open up. He spent his holidays from university working at Kentucky Fried Chicken.

The children had infinitely more meaningful choices than their father, despite the fact that their formal political freedoms under the new regime of President Suharto were not necessarily any greater than under Sukarno. But what mattered was that, from day to day, they could wear what they wanted, speak as they wanted, be gay or straight or bisexual as they wanted, and, if the civil service and military didn't like it, they could choose from plenty of jobs in the private sector instead. Many political theorists argued that it would be precisely this emerging class of private-sector middle-class people that would go on to press for greater formal political freedoms and indeed this did happen in Indonesia. However, the more fundamental point is that the freedom to choose who you work for gives you a wide range of other daily freedoms—regardless of what the constitution says or whether you have a vote in an occasional election.

So the presence of business in a country can contribute to 'development as freedom' in far more profound ways than simply increasing income or giving access to consumer goods. This might not be something you want to trumpet to your host government; in Indonesia, President Suharto opened up the economy solely for the financial benefits and was surprised and angered by the accompanying loss of political and social control. But it is an important argument to make when talking to donor agencies and anti-globalisation advocates.

The process of community consultation

One important way in which business can contribute to 'development as freedom' is by how you manage the consultation process if, for example, you are building a project such as a mine or road that will affect or displace local people. For many years, the traditional approach was to ignore the problem altogether, but most multinational companies now recognise that they're unlikely to get away with that. However, the modern alternative, of consulting 'community leaders', may not be significantly better, as it is likely to reinforce existing authoritarian structures.

If you want to share our scepticism about community leaders, ask yourself who your own 'community leader' is? Who are you happy to have speak on your behalf? We bet you don't answer 'the local mayor'—some self-serving, self-appointed busybody who got the job only because no one else could be bothered to stand. The journalist Tim Luckhurst put it this way in *The Times* on 3 August 2005:

> There is a fellow in my street who runs a 'community association'. His neighbours have declined to join, but still he purports to represent us. The council encourages him because it is easier to negotiate with one self-appointed leader than with assorted individuals with distinct concerns. That, of course, is the point of communities. They are a convenient fiction. The incessant talk of

faith, local and ethnic communities is part of a drive to diminish individuality and render people compliant. Nobody has joined these communities. Their puffed up leaders are useful fools with no mandate at all.

We've certainly come across our fair share of rather grand 'community leaders' who've learned a bit of development or corporate vocabulary and use it to live a good life attending seminars and conferences, but when you talk to local people they often ask, 'why the hell are you dealing with him?'[13] The honest answer might be 'because it's easy'. But if you're not prepared to talk to a wide range of local people too then, of course, you have no idea whether this person is their legitimate representative or not and you can have no confidence in this person's advice or agreement.

Amartya Sen makes the point that you need to consult widely, not simply because it produces better results but also because the process is an important end in itself. He says:

> Such processes as participation in political decisions and social choice cannot be seen as being—at best—among the *means* to development (through, say, their contribution to economic growth), but have to be understood as constitutive parts of the *ends* of development in themselves.[14]

Only through consultation can we be sure that the results of development are things that people genuinely have reason to value (including the right to be consulted), rather than just imperfect measures such as increased income which, as we have identified, are only partial indicators of freedom and well-being.

This consultative approach offers some useful signposts when considering the potential for business activities to destroy traditional ways of life. This is currently something of a sterile argument. The bluff, pragmatic businessman says: 'it's better to be rich and happy than impoverished and traditional' (not an argument he would make about a factory development in the fields behind his own house at home in the West). The anti-globalisation advocate wants to hang on to traditional ways of life at all costs, even when they create disease and injustice.

13 Once in Pakistan, we attended a women's group constituted by donors for consultation purposes, which consisted entirely of men. They politely told us that the women were, of course, at home doing the cooking so couldn't come.

14 A. Sen, *Development as Freedom* (Oxford: Oxford University Press, 1999).

Sen, elegant and wise as ever, puts it as follows:

> There is an inescapable problem involved in deciding what to choose if and when it turns out that some parts of tradition cannot be maintained along with economic or social changes that may be needed for other reasons. It is a choice that the people involved have to face and assess. The choice is neither closed (as many development apologists seem to suggest), nor is it one for the elite 'guardians' of tradition to settle (as many development sceptics seem to assume). If a traditional way of life has to be sacrificed to escape grinding poverty or minuscule longevity, then it is for the people directly involved who must have the opportunity to participate in deciding what should be chosen.
>
> The real conflict is between the basic value that the people must be allowed to decide freely what traditions they wish or do not wish to follow; and the insistence that established traditions be followed (no matter what) or, alternatively, people must obey the decisions by religious or secular authorities who enforce real or imagined traditions.
>
> In the freedom-oriented perspective the liberty of all to participate in deciding what traditions to observe cannot be ruled out by the national or local 'guardians'—neither by the ayatollahs (or other religious authorities), nor by political rulers (or governmental dictators), nor by cultural 'experts' (domestic or foreign).

This is a simple and attractive policy for companies to follow. They do not even begin to try to choose between a complex mix of religious, political, social and economic values all tied in with questions of tradition and authority. Instead they stick to one simple precept—that the local people must be consulted. This will save an awful lot of time and money, and will fundamentally contribute to development as freedom in a way that development people are beginning to understand and value.

Conclusions

Companies need to communicate their activities in ways that are relevant to the ambitions of their host country. In Chapter 9 on reputation, we discuss how to do this when communicating with non-experts such as the public, local business people and politicians. In this chapter, we've aimed to capture what economists, development experts and relevant civil servants will be thinking about poverty and development, and we describe how your business activities can be made relevant to this audience.

Your direct effect on income is important and is worth measuring because it is a widely used measure in national and global development policy. But you should not underestimate the indirect effects, which are becoming increasingly valued for development. These range from the economic side-effects of skills transfer, technology and creation of a business infrastructure through to political and social empowerment for your employees and your local community.

Follow-up questions

How does your host country measure poverty and what does it plan to do about it? What does the Poverty Reduction Strategy Paper say? How does your business contribute to those aims?

How many people do you or your direct suppliers employ who formerly earned less than the equivalent of $1 (or $2) a day in purchasing power parity terms? Have you told your head office this?

How does your business support better access for poor people to goods and services?

Do your consultations with local people reinforce or reduce repression? How legitimate are the 'community leaders' you deal with?

How does your business support greater autonomy for poor people? How well do you communicate that?

Further reading

Development as Freedom by Amartya Sen, published by Oxford University Press in 1999, is the fundamental text we draw on in this chapter. It's packed full of material, not all of which will be relevant to business readers, but it's the essential text if you're really interested in this aspect of poverty.

Dissent on Development: Studies and Debates in Development Economics by Peter Bauer was published in the 1970s (initially by Weidenfeld & Nicolson in 1971, followed by a revised edition in 1972 by Harvard University Press), but remains a fundamental text if you treasure personal initiative and the private sector, and are suspicious of government intervention and large aid programmes. It's not an easy read, but is useful ammunition if your development friends try to assume the moral high ground.

Poverty Reduction Strategy Papers are available from the World Bank and IMF. As of March 2006, they were available for free download from the IMF website (www.imf. org/external/np/prsp/prsp.asp). They are a valuable source of economic data and are key for anyone attempting to make themselves relevant to a country's development plans.

The Penn World Table gives a host of economic data, including purchasing power parity figures, for every country. As of March 2006, it was available at no cost and with an easy-to-use interface at http://pwt.econ.upenn.edu.

For links to these resources and other relevant material, go to www.makepovertybusiness.com.

4

Poverty and inefficiency traps

> " Agreements are often not made when they could have been to the advantage of all parties. Agreements are often made that are inefficient: others could have been made that would have been preferred by all parties. "
>
> Source: Howard Raiffa, *The Art and Science of Negotiation* (Cambridge, MA: Belknap Press, 1982).

What stops companies doing business with poor people? If it is all so obvious, why doesn't it happen already? Why do we need a book to tell us what to do?

This chapter is all about identifying the subtle systems that stop people making mutually beneficial agreements. Most of the work on this has been done by development economists who look at it from the perspective of poor people—what traps them into unemployment, lack of business opportunities, insufficient credit to operate at efficient scale? We look at this from the other perspective and so we call them 'inefficiency traps' rather than poverty traps—systems that prevent companies from doing business efficiently with poor people. The solutions to these traps rarely involve money and often depend simply on increasing one's ability to form trusting relation-ships and to commit to agreements.

One of the apparent mysteries about the process of opening up to free mar-kets and foreign investment is that the process tends to reinforce rather than undermine the status quo. You would expect that the old elites of peo-ple who got rich from land or political power would be replaced by entre-preneurs with business skills. But the evidence from South-East Asia and Russia is that old political and aristocratic elites thrive on the new opportu-nities.[15] The poor might get slightly richer, but rarely change places with the old rich.

This is a dangerous situation for international companies, who quite unwittingly find themselves tarred by the sometimes disappointing results of capitalism. It's bad for their reputation because it associates them with propping up privileged classes or ethnic groups and delivering few benefits for the poor. And it's bad for profits because it restricts the number of peo-ple they can deal with as suppliers, distributors or customers. Poverty/inef-ficiency traps are the key to explaining much of this, and a company that understands them can increase its bargaining power and improve its repu-tation with local people, governments and development agencies.

Of course, there's nothing new about companies tackling poverty traps. In the 19th century in Britain, successful business people such as the Rown-tree and Cadbury families provided their employees with nutrition, hous-ing and health facilities. There was undoubtedly a strong moral and phil-anthropic quality to these interventions, but there was also a clear element of self-interest. A poor person paid a wage that is too low to buy sufficient nutrition is too weak to work hard and so cannot credibly promise to do the job properly. The company may be offering a marginally higher wage than the alternative of subsistence farming, but the potential employee cannot take up the offer with any expectation of being able to do the job. Offering a higher wage and other help with health and nutrition allows the company to employ a fitter, more productive individual. This is a simple example of an 'efficiency wage', where it is directly in the company's interest to offer significantly higher wages than the prevailing market rate.

While many companies may not need to worry these days about the basic nutrition of their employees, the thinking can still be applied to overcom-ing the other barriers that poor people face when seeking to do business

---

15   E.g. T. Gerber and M. Hunt, 'More Shock than Therapy: Market Transition, Em-ployment and Income in Russia, 1991–1995', *American Journal of Sociology* 104.1 (July 1998).

with multinational companies. The primary reason for doing so is based on a commonplace of business strategy—the larger your pool of potential suppliers, employees and customers, the stronger your bargaining power. But such thinking will also allow companies to tap into the increasing interest in development organisations and governments in 'pro-poor' growth. The Oxford economist Professor Stefan Dercon describes the debate as follows:

> Traditional textbook economics teaching emphasised that equity considerations could and had to be considered separately from efficiency considerations. The simple argument was that the economy, when left to its own devices, could achieve the most efficient outcome . . . Equity considerations have little role to play in this view—in fact, any measure favouring the poor is considered costly: redistribution reduces economic incentives and performance. Okun described redistribution famously to be like carrying money from the rich to the poor in 'a leaky bucket'. Voltaire's Dr Pangloss would have been proud of this view: do not try to touch the distribution of resources, or the best possible outcome is not achieved. In short, there is a fundamental trade-off between efficiency and equity . . .
>
> Of course, many economists have for many years argued that the underlying assumptions of these theorems are fundamentally flawed: market failures abound. Furthermore, with market failures, the principle of interventions that may be efficiency-enhancing is well established. During the last few decades, economists have shown that imperfections such as asymmetric information, uncertainty and externalities mean that there are, at least theoretically, always interventions that will be able to make many better-off without making anyone worse-off.
>
> A subset of these interventions is of particular relevance for the poor. These are related to market failures that specifically hurt the poor, and interact with their living conditions in such a way as to exacerbate their poverty. They do this by reducing the efficiency by which the poor use their assets, while leaving the rich largely unaffected. In some cases, these market failures may even lead to poverty traps, equilibrium outcomes of poor living conditions from which the poor, using their own resources, cannot escape. Interventions focused on the poor—redistribution—would in that case lead to efficiency increases for the poor. They may in fact also increase overall efficiency. In other words, there is no efficiency-

equity trade-off: rather, redistributive interventions, designed in particular ways, could increase overall efficiency . . .[16]

There is a clear connection here between the argument that economists are making about the economy as a whole and the argument that we are making about individual companies. Dercon argues that, if a government or a development agency leaves everything to the market, they will be missing opportunities for 'win–win' interventions—for example, by providing credit to poor people to allow them to operate at efficient scale. Similarly, we argue that companies cannot rely just on the prevailing market conditions either. They may decide to intervene in certain areas where the market fails in order to achieve 'win–win' results for both sides. The point is that governments and companies are not just transferring money to the poor—which is fine if we are interested in equity but less justifiable in terms of efficiency—but that we are actually creating new value that can be shared between the poor and the government or company. Joseph Rowntree decided not simply to pay the market wage and put up with ineffective workers, but instead to intervene with social security programmes to increase his workers' efficiency. In a perfect world, he wouldn't have needed to (governments would have intervened or workers would have solved their own problems), but the world wasn't perfect and Rowntree chose some selective intervention to improve the market conditions for his operations. Companies that understand these questions can offer governments and development agencies not only the growth that comes from foreign direct investment, but the 'pro-poor growth' that has become a Holy Grail.

We might even argue that the existence in some countries of growth that doesn't help the poor is simply because companies are missing opportunities to achieve efficiency *and* equity, and host governments and development agencies aren't strong enough or smart enough to prod them to do so. Development economists and governments may become more confident about the pro-poor benefits of foreign direct investment once companies get cleverer and realise the disadvantages in cost and reputation of unwittingly channelling all of the benefits of their presence into the hands of a fortunate few.

16 S. Dercon, *Poverty Traps and Development: The Equity–Efficiency Trade-Off Revisited* (paper prepared for the Conference on Growth, Inequality and Poverty, organised by the Agence française de développement and the European Development Research Network [EUDN], September 2003; www.economics.ox.ac.uk/members/ stefan.dercon/poverty%20traps.pdf, 8 March 2006).

Self-fulfilling discrimination

Let's start with a simple example of an inefficiency trap. Suppose there are two types of people in the world, blue and green, of equal capability and decency. For some reason, the idea has got around that green people are discriminated against. When greens apply for jobs at blue companies, they do not really expect to succeed because they expect to be the victim of discrimination. So they indiscriminately fire off applications without bothering to match themselves to the specific job requirements and they don't prepare for the interview. Inevitably, their expectations are met and they don't get the job. The greens get confirmation that they are discriminated against, the blue company gets confirmation that greens are rubbish and so therefore shouldn't be encouraged to come for future interviews, and the vicious circle spirals downward.

The system doesn't suit either party. Greens make the apparently rational decision not to invest much time or money in applying for a job or securing a supply contract, but as a result they lose out on real opportunities. Blues don't identify the greens' real potential and are left competing for a narrow pool of blue employees and suppliers, who are thus able to charge more for their services.

Let's drop the political correctness and make the obvious point that we're talking about ethnic groups and nationalities. If businesses give the impression (however unwittingly) that they are not interested in dealing with people from a specific group, then they will miss out on potential employees and suppliers. Worse, their assumptions about certain groups will become self-fulfilling.

Fortunately, this problem is relatively easy to overcome. By committing to a programme of diversity and promising to take applications from certain groups seriously, a company can tap into a new pool of under-utilised, low-cost talent.

BP's role in developing local business in Azerbaijan

** BP's leadership role in developing local businesses and encouraging economic diversity is supported through the Enterprise Centre (EC). Analysis of current barriers to local business pointed to poor supplier awareness of future opportunities, poor BP awareness of supplier capability, limited supplier competency and language barriers. The EC has been addressing these areas and significantly improved BP's connection to suppliers and other stakeholders.

The Enterprise Centre training programme has proved to be very popular within the local business community in Azerbaijan, who see the value and importance of improvement in these areas. Training courses on HSE, business ethics, various aspects of doing business with oil companies and general business training have already been provided at the Enterprise Centre. And other comprehensive training and education programmes are planned in support of local SMEs which will help them equip themselves with necessary capabilities to be more widely involved in BP operated projects."

Source: BP Enterprise Centre Report 2004; for further details see www.ecbaku.com.

BP's large and growing operations in Azerbaijan have been supported by the foundation of an Enterprise Centre to facilitate links with local businesses. The EC, co-funded by BP and partners Azerbaijan International Operating Company (AIOC), Baku Tbilisi Ceyhan (BTC) and Shah Deniz, aims to increase local sourcing in all areas of BP's operations from the core business of oil extraction through to support services such as catering, website design and production of promotional items.

The EC works with local businesses to help them learn about supply opportunities and to develop the capabilities to win the contract. Information provision on contract opportunities includes an email subscription service which, by the end of 2004, had 2,600 subscribers and a website (www.ecbaku.com) with 15,000 visitors per month. The EC provides initial information, training and advice to budding bidders but there is no magic wand or philanthropy involved. The EC's client companies ultimately have to win normal competitive tenders directly with BP's operating companies and must offer a better price and quality package than other local and international competitors.

The EC also offers a consultancy service to BP and other multinational companies operating in Azerbaijan to identify opportunities for efficiency gains through local sourcing. It then offers market research services to identify competent local suppliers who can fill the gap. In 2004, just over half of its requests were from within BP, the rest coming from other international and local companies.

In some cases where the wider development benefits are clear, the EC will partner with development agencies such as the World Bank's International Finance Corporation (IFC) on specific projects to develop local capabilities.

In 2004, BP spent a total of $57 million with local small and medium-sized enterprises (SMEs), an increase of 19% on the 2003 total. We should remember that, after the EC's initial pump-priming work, the decision to spend that money locally rather than internationally would have been made on the sound business criteria that the local offer was cheaper and/or better-quality, indicating a substantial efficiency saving to BP. The EC's annual running costs of $250,000 are currently funded entirely by BP and its partners, but there is a plan to start charging external companies for some of the EC's consultancy services in order to achieve sustainability. The EC also plans to offer advice to similar operations in other countries and has already been exchanging ideas with BP in Angola and AGIP in Kazakhstan.

The Enterprise Centre has an important wider role as a catalyst in allowing local companies to overcome barriers of lack of trust, lack of information and language gaps with the international business community as a whole and, ultimately, has a much greater development effect than simply increasing BP's local supplier base. For example, the EC's 'seal of approval' on a local agricultural company, Agro Yurd, helped it to win contracts with the international catering company Gama, McDonald's and Radisson, and the EC is now working with the IFC to expand Agro Yurd's capabilities in organic farming.

The EC identifies more efficient local procurement for BP as its primary aim, though acknowledges the secondary motivation of improved local and international reputation. As the EC report proudly says:

" The objectives and activities of the EC have been widely advertised within Azerbaijan through press releases, the opening event, newspaper coverage and open house sessions. The international community has been advised through Share Fair events in Baku, Tbilisi and Aberdeen and publicity at the Caspian Oil & Gas Show. EC visitors have included the UK Energy Minister; our JV partners; BP Vice Presidents; Azeri Government Ministers; trade missions from UK, Italy, France, Denmark; the IFC president; Prince Michael of Kent; and many others. "

The problem of lack of trust

The self-fulfilling discrimination trap is a neat theoretical example of a general practical problem for multinational companies—a lack of trust between foreigners and locals. Local people don't know which multinational companies to trust to take them seriously, so don't invest the time and money to offer goods and services. Multinational companies, operating in a new and unfamiliar environment where legal guarantees may be weak, don't know which locals to trust to be competent and honest suppliers. So they either import all their labour and supplies from abroad or rely on a very narrow range of 'usual suspect' locals, who can monopolise trade with foreign companies and charge accordingly. Either way, the multinational overpays.

The economists Chaim Fershtman and Uri Gneezy used a nice game theory experiment to test the problems of establishing trust with 'foreign' strangers.[17] They asked a mixture of Ashkenazi and Eastern Jews within Israel to play a game in which both players could benefit by forming a trusting relationship (Eastern Jews are traditionally relatively under-privileged in Israel). They found that Ashkenazi Jews could form mutually beneficial trusting relationships with Ashkenazi strangers but were unable to do so with Eastern strangers. This was despite the fact that Ashkenazi players felt warmth towards Eastern Jews and had no 'taste for discrimination' and, furthermore, that any stereotypes were inaccurate—Eastern Jews did not in general play the game any differently to Ashkenazim when offered the chance to do so. The problem was that Ashkenazi Jews found all Eastern Jews relatively 'foreign' and could not discriminate within that to find the specific individuals they felt they could trust.

Many investors overcome the inability to trust foreign strangers by using personal ties to do business. The economist Henry Yeung studied these mechanisms in a study of the behaviour of Hong Kong firms investing in South-East Asia in which he asked 111 Hong Kong-based multinationals to name the single most important mechanism for establishing a South-East Asian operation.[18] The top two responses were 'the existence of a reliable local partner to set up the operation' (28%) and the statement that 'personal relations are important in establishing overseas operations' (20%). The judgement of reliability or the establishment of a personal tie often

---

17 C. Fershtman and U. Gneezy, 'Discrimination in a Segmented Society: An Experimental Approach', *Quarterly Journal of Economics*, February 2001: 351-77.

18 H.W.-C. Yeung, 'Business Networks and Transnational Corporations: A Study of Hong Kong Firms in the ASEAN region', *Economic Geography* 73.1 (January 1997): 1ff.

depended on ethnic similarity or direct family connections. The mechanism of 'a well-developed corporate procedure to set up overseas corporations' was mentioned by only 5% of respondents.

" Virtually every commercial transaction has within itself an element of trust."

Source: Professor Kenneth Arrow, 'Gifts and Exchanges', in E.S. Phelps (ed.), *Altruism, Morality and Economic Theory* (New York: Russell Sage Foundation, 1975): 24.

These mechanisms tend to lead to the emergence of a small set of 'usual suspects' who are able to establish trusting relationships with multinational companies. They often use ethnic or personal ties, or some existing political power or wealth, to establish their first relationship. They then use this track record to establish further business relationships in widely diversified areas. Their skills are often solely in establishing relationships rather than in any specific business field; there is evidence for this in many studies that show that companies in developing countries tend to be much more diversified than in the developed world. Such charmed groups of people are often extremely small and once established they become self-sustaining—the economist David Kowaleski found that the top 46 business families in the Philippines were connected to 90% of all Japanese investment into the country and responsible for 237 of the top 1,000 corporations in the country.[19] Unsurprisingly, he found that the greater the multinational domination of developing Asian economies, the greater the share of income received by the top 5% of all income earners. Of course, companies don't intend for any of this to happen, but through this simple poverty/inefficiency trap, they become associated with supporting the status quo and doing little for 'the people'.

Having such a narrow range of potential suppliers is bad for poverty alleviation and bad for multinational companies. The system tends to concentrate the benefits of development in the hands of a small group of people and does little to increase opportunity in society as a whole. Multinational companies have to deal with a small group of people who have no specific skills, but have a strong bargaining power because there are few apparent alternatives. It would be in everyone's interest, except for the self-sustaining local elite, to widen the range of trusted locals. And it would be in the specific

19   D. Kowaleski, 'Transnational Corporations and Asian Inequality', *Pacific Affairs* 60.4 (Winter 1987–88): 578-95.

interests of individual companies to do more to accurately identify the locals whom they can really trust rather than rely on inaccurate measures such as ethnic group, personal ties or track records in unrelated industries.

BP's Enterprise Centre in Azerbaijan represents an attempt to overcome some of these problems. First of all it represents a visible commitment by BP and partners to local supply. This encourages locals to trust BP to take them seriously, so that they will invest time and money in preparing proposals. Secondly, it helps local people to overcome superficial weaknesses, such as lack of language skills or lack of information about opportunities, to allow BP and its partners to accurately identify those suppliers with relevant skills. The development of a wider range of local suppliers greatly strengthens BP's negotiating hand when dealing with expensive foreign suppliers or the small number of existing local suppliers, and can only be good for its business.

This is a classic example of how to cut through the apparent conflict in thinking about poverty alleviation and business, which is that companies want to pay less and local people want to charge more. In this case, paying less to a new entrant does more for equitable economic development and poverty alleviation than overpaying an existing monopolist.

The 'hold-up' problem

There's one apparently curious feature of the EC system. Why do they offer it, for free, to other multinational companies? There might be clear philanthropic benefits to local suppliers and the other multinationals, but what's the business case for BP and the other funding partners? Why have your staff working on other people's supply problems when they could be working on your own?

The answer brings us to a second problem for multinationals seeking local suppliers—the 'hold-up' problem—which happens when a supplier invests a significant amount in order to supply a single customer. The problem arises because this gives the customer unlimited bargaining power over the supplier, who has no alternative customers and therefore has no choice but to be bargained down to marginal cost. Of course, this is great for the customer when it happens, but potential suppliers can anticipate the problem and so don't bother to invest in the first place. Ultimately, therefore, the customer suffers; the supplier cannot be persuaded to make the investments necessary to provide the supplies because the customer can't credibly promise not to exploit the resulting relationship.

This is far from being only a theoretical problem. For example, there is evidence that Japanese motor manufacturers repeatedly abused 'one-to-one' relationships with suppliers in South-East Asia in order to drive down supply prices. The suppliers have learned their lesson and won't make the same mistake again.

There are various solutions to the problem. The best is obviously for the potential supplier to have a range of potential customers available. This is clearly the rationale for the Enterprise Centre to work with other potential buyers; it gives suppliers the confidence to invest, knowing that they will not lose all bargaining power. It also allows suppliers to operate at an efficient scale, thus cutting costs and creating a win–win situation.

Even where it is not possible to develop additional customers, a multinational company can try to reassure potential suppliers that they will not exploit the relationship. A public commitment to developing local sourcing can make it significantly harder for a multinational to renege on a deal later on. A multinational company might agree to sign a longer-term legal agreement than would be common in their home country, or might even provide legal and negotiation expertise to the supplier. It may seem counter-intuitive to deliberately strengthen a supplier's bargaining power and weaken your own, and indeed in a mature market economy with a wide choice of potential suppliers it would be madness. But, in an immature economy with a dearth of local suppliers, the choice is not between a fair deal or an advantageous deal, but between a fair deal and no deal at all.

●● In general, advanced economies have large pools of seasoned market intermediaries and effective contract-enforcing mechanisms, whereas less-developed economies have unskilled intermediaries and less-effective legal systems. Because the services provided by intermediaries either aren't available in emerging markets or aren't very sophisticated, corporations can't smoothly transfer the strategies they employ in their home countries to those emerging markets . . .

In the United States, McDonald's has outsourced most of its supply chain operations. But when it tried to move into Russia in 1990, the company was unable to find local suppliers. The fast-food chain asked several of its European vendors to step up, but they weren't interested. Instead of giving up, McDonald's decided to go it alone. With the help of its joint venture partner, the Moscow City Administration, the company identified some Russian farmers and bakers it could work with. It imported cattle from Holland and russet potatoes from America, brought in agricultural specialists from Canada and Europe to improve the farmers' management practices, and advanced the farmers money so that they could invest in better seeds and equipment.**

Source: Tarun Khanna, Krishna Palepu and Jayant Sinha, 'Strategies that Fit Emerging Markets', *Harvard Business Review*, June 2005.

** Companies sometimes try to apply a tried-and-true strategy without realizing that they are operating in markets that require a different approach. Even such a world-beater at execution as Wal-Mart, for instance, has sometimes made some missteps because of culture. One example: When Wal-Mart first moved in to Brazil, it tried to lay down terms with suppliers in the same way it does in the U.S., where it carries huge weight in the market. Suppliers simply refused to play, and the company was forced to re-evaluate its strategy.**

Source: 'Three Reasons Why Good Strategies Fail: Execution, Execution . . .', Knowledge@Wharton; http://knowledge.wharton.upenn.edu/article/1252.cfm, 9 March 2005.

The value of networks

Perhaps some of this seems utopian. It must be obvious that one should look for the 'perfect' local supplier with relevant skills rather than choose someone because you know them or they've been successful in other fields. But is it feasible in practice? In a foreign environment with imperfect information where there are few companies with solid track records, perhaps the time and cost of searching for and testing the 'right' supplier outweighs the benefit of finding him or her. The second-best of using the most obvious existing partner perhaps makes more sense when search costs are high.

** Multinational companies may be unaware of the availability of viable suppliers, or they may find it too costly to use them as sources of inputs. In developing countries, policies may be required to compensate for weak financial markets or weak institutions like vocational schools, training institutes, technology support centres, R&D and testing laboratories and the like. Well-designed government intervention can raise the benefits and reduce the costs of using domestic suppliers.

The role of policy is most significant where there is an 'information gap' on the part of both buyers and suppliers about linkage opportunities, a 'capability gap' between the requirements of buyers and the supply capacity of suppliers and where the costs and risks for setting up linkages or deepening them can be reduced."

Source: UN Conference on Trade and Development, *World Investment Report 2001: Promoting Linkages* (Geneva: United Nations Publications, 2001).

Fortunately, some solutions are emerging to this problem. In addition to the intervention by governments and development agencies recommended by the UN Conference of Trade and Development (UNCTAD), independent intermediaries are also springing up who can search for and audit potential partners and spread the cost across a range of customers. Effectively, they are bringing economies of scale to the problem of establishing trust between multinationals and locals. One good example of this is Innovasia, set up by the INSEAD business school (www.insead.edu) from its Singapore campus. Innovasia acts as the centre of a network that links multinationals with innovative Asian companies and entrepreneurs. It researches the capabilities of a wide range of companies throughout the region, and shares the cost of doing so between its multinational members who benefit from analysis and introductions.

Once again, there is an opportunity here for multinational companies to increase efficiency and contribute to development without spending much of their own money. As a country manager, could you use your convening power and authority to persuade a local business school, university or development body to start linking your company, and others, to local suppliers? The development arguments are clear and have been set out in UNCTAD's 2001 report.[20] The business arguments for applying economies of scale to search costs should also be obvious and are already being exploited by initiatives such as the Innovasia network.

On a larger scale, the option of clubbing together with other multinationals to form something like BP's Enterprise Centre is an attractive option which offers more efficient procurement and improved reputation for limited initial investment. And, if none of this is attractive, at least a public

20 UN Conference on Trade and Development, *World Investment Report 2001: Promoting Linkages* (Geneva: United Nations Publications, 2001).

commitment to taking local business seriously is a cost-free start to this process, which may overcome the inefficiency trap of self-perpetuating discrimination.

The problem of lack of credit

••While off-farm activities are generally hailed as an important route for enrichment, access to some of the simplest activities, such as livestock rearing for milk products, trading, small shops or some handicrafts, require relatively important investments. Empirical research in both Tanzania and Ethiopia, where off-farm income is essential in many marginal areas, found that those with least assets restricted their off-farm activities to gathering activities (selling dungcakes or firewood) or handicrafts without substantial start-up costs such as weaving, while others managed to enter into much higher return off-farm activities. In Western Tanzania, where cattle provide an important high-return activity, one mature cow cost about 50 percent of median crop income. In Ethiopia, the median investment needed to enter into charcoal making, dungcake collection, weaving, or food processing—activities with relatively low returns—was 0–20 birr (up to €3). More lucrative activities, such as starting a shop, trading livestock, or providing transport services, required 300–550 birr (€45–€80). A mature cow costs about 400 birr (€60). These are large sums in an economy in which mean per adult income is less than €200 a year.••

Source: Professor Stefan Dercon, *Poverty Traps and Development: The Equity–Efficiency Trade-off Revisited* (paper prepared for the Conference on Growth, Inequality and Poverty organised by the Agence française de développement and the European Development Research Network [EUDN], September 2003; www.economics.ox.ac.uk/members/stefan.dercon/poverty%20traps.pdf, 8 March 2006).

In a perfect world, if you had a profitable opportunity you could borrow money to pursue it. But of course the world is imperfect and potential investors/lenders can find it difficult to trust you.

- They lack information about whether you are trustworthy
- They have less information than you on whether the opportunity is indeed profitable

- They find it difficult to monitor whether you use the money responsibly

- They have difficulty in enforcing repayment

In the developed world, we deal with some of these problems via a sophisticated legal system, but even this is not perfect and most credit systems are supplemented by a demand for collateral or evidence of an existing track record of credit repayments.

All of these imperfections create a poverty trap for people who might want to become your suppliers, distributors or customers. If you have no assets, how do you provide collateral? And, if you have no collateral, how do you begin to establish a track record? In some countries with under-developed legal systems, even those people who do own reasonable assets, such as a house or land, have trouble proving their proper legal ownership and therefore cannot 'collateralise' their assets into a form that would be accepted by an investor as a proper guarantee.

So, if you are already rich, you can borrow money for profitable new projects and get even richer. But, if you are poor, you have no access to credit so you are unable to invest to operate at efficient scale and you are left carrying out some low-investment, low-return activity that doesn't create value for anyone.

At this stage you may object that, if such poverty traps are so all-pervasive, how did any country ever get out of them? How could any industrial revolution happen if everyone who is poor now has no way of ever getting rich?

Historians of the British industrial revolution have studied the problem and concluded that entrepreneurs overcame the lack of a proper legal system or proper collateral by exploiting their social ties and existing wealth (often derived from land). The economic historian Crouzet says: 'a large majority of industrialists came from well-to-do families, which could supply them with some capital to start in business and which also had useful networks of connections in their communities',[21] while Postan adds:

> that in founding their enterprises the pioneers of the factory system had to draw almost entirely on their private savings, or on the assistance of friends, may not strike us as strange. But that throughout their subsequent operations, even after their ventures had proved successful, they should still have found it impossible

---

21 François Crouzet, *The First Industrialists: The Problem of Origins* (Cambridge, UK: Cambridge University Press, 1985).

> to raise new capital, except among acquaintances and friends, is very significant.[22]

We are back to the problem of trust. If you belong to an exalted social or ethnic group, you already have the trusting relationships to be able to borrow money and to exploit new business opportunities. But, if you come from a less well-connected group, you have no route out. Once again, the opening of markets and the presence of foreign investors will quite unwittingly tend to reinforce existing wealth rather than create new opportunities for poor people.

What does this mean for multinational companies? The first thing to say is that we are not recommending that everyone rushes into poor people's banking. If it were easy to overcome the problems of giving credit to people who don't have collateral or track records, then many companies would have done it by now. The traps are real and difficult to overcome, rather than the result of deliberately obtuse policies by 'evil' commercial banks.

Micro-credit companies tried to compensate for the lack of legal systems and proper collateral by exploiting the power of shame and stigma in tight-knit societies. In the classic micro-credit model, loans are made to groups of women who will ostracise any member who reneges on the deal. As a result, repayment rates tend to be extremely high. However, the shine is beginning to come off these models because they are difficult to scale up. It is a labour-intensive activity requiring good local understanding to exploit social ties in this way and not something that is easy for multinational companies to do. Few micro-credit operations have made the transition from being philanthropic social movements to being efficient, large-scale businesses offering acceptable rates of financial return.

All of this probably means that you wouldn't want to enter the micro-credit business unless you can find some imaginative solutions to the age-old problems of credit. But there still may be opportunities for co-operation between multinationals, with their profit motive, and micro-credit outfits, with their philanthropic concerns. The profitable opportunity for the multinational is to use its existing knowledge to help poor people on one side and micro-credit and banking outfits on the other to overcome the lack of trust between them.

---

22 M.M. Postan, 'Recent Trends in the Accumulation of Capital', *Economic History Review* 6 (1935); repr. in F. Crouzet (ed.), *Capital Formation in the Industrial Revolution* (London: Methuen, 1972).

If you have used the mechanisms outlined at the beginning of this chapter to identify suppliers or distributors that you believe are trustworthy and competent, why not use that knowledge to help them secure credit.

- Can you give them your 'seal of approval' and introduce them to your local banker or micro-credit outfit?

- Can you give them some sort of guaranteed purchase contract, subject to them achieving proper quality, which they can take to the bank instead of physical collateral?

- Can you promise to share your monitoring information with the bank?

Remember that credit outfits and banks are always looking for people whom they can safely invest in, and at no cost to yourself you can point them in the direction of the people you want to do business with. The simple first step is to go and talk to the banks and the micro-credit outfits, ask them who they're interested in investing in, and consider whether any of your potential suppliers, distributors or customers fit the bill. Conversely, they may have already identified and funded reliable local businesses that could become your supplier.

For example, Unilever in Bangladesh has partnered with local banks to help its product distributors to gain access to finance that helps get their business started and keep them going and which helps, in the end, to sell Unilever products (in some places, this is called channel finance). What Unilever had found before was that distributors and potential distributors of its products were having enormous difficulty obtaining finance. This was largely due to the insistence of banks on complex forms of collateral, which the would-be entrepreneurs did not have. The banks were also worried about a lack of reliable information about would-be borrowers' activities. Through a partnership with local banks, Unilever offered to supply information to the banks on the amount of goods being supplied to their distributors (copies of the invoices) and also offered limited guarantees on loans made against those amounts. In this way, banks felt more assured in their lending, the distributors (small, mostly rural business people) obtained ready access to working capital, and Unilever's product distribution improved markedly.

Despite the misperception that capital shortages are holding back development, banks across east, west and sub-Saharan Africa are actually flush with money. Yet they refuse to lend it to those who can do the most with it—millions of disenfranchised, small-scale African entrepreneurs who could lift Africa out of poverty if given half a chance.

Local African banks have to develop the confidence and the investment mechanisms to shift away from lending solely on the basis of a trading record with 100 per cent collateral. Instead, they need to begin providing finance secured against the entrepreneur's business plan and above all against a belief in the management team taking the investment forward . . .

To help bring this about, the Shell Foundation has been piloting commercially viable ways of channelling mentoring and financing to large numbers of smaller companies in need of early-stage capital of less than $1 million. The model enables local African banks to invest in the SME sector by outsourcing risk to a specialist fund manager, in this case co-established by the Shell Foundation.""

Source: Kurt Hoffman, Director of the Shell Foundation, 'Lack of Investment is the Tragedy in Africa', *Financial Times*, 10 June 2005; available at www.shellfoundation.org/index.php?articleID=36.

"". . . what was inadequate was not the quantity of stored up wealth, but its behaviour . . . conduits to connect savings with the wheels of industry were few and meagre.""

Source: M.M. Postan writing in 1935 about the British Industrial Revolution.

The problem of uninsured risk

While many companies have started to go off the micro-credit model as a viable business opportunity, development economists have also begun to question some of its effects on the lives of poor people. The idea of using social stigma as a replacement for a functioning legal system is ingenious, but it does have drawbacks. We grew up in the 1970s in Britain, and were always being told that we had to be nice to the local bank manager and develop a track record with him if we ever wanted to get a mortgage. It gave a rather boring man disproportionate social power in the village. How much nicer it is now to be bombarded with offers of credit from a variety of providers, all using a legal system rather than some measure of social worth to guarantee their loans, and how nice it is to have suppliers trying to convince the customer rather than vice versa. The old system of using social ties instead of the rule of law tended to reinforce existing social and class structures.

The less glib point for poor people in developing countries is that the availability of credit increases their risk only if there is no system of forgiveness and no system of insurance in place for those unlucky enough to be unable to repay. In developed countries, we have a system of bankruptcy because we want people to take risks to start businesses, and so we do not want the punishment to be too harsh if they fail. Bankruptcy offers a period of purdah followed by an opportunity to wipe the slate clean and start again. Sadly, social networks have no such systems of automatic forgiveness. A person who fails to make a repayment, perhaps through no fault of his or her own, can be ostracised forever, cut off not only from further loans but all forms of social and commercial life. This is a powerful disincentive to take the loan in the first place and a disproportionate punishment for an honest risk-taker operating in a volatile environment.

In developed countries, we deal with business risks through the bankruptcy system but also through savings and insurance. The trap for poor people is that they rarely have effective savings and insurance mechanisms open to them. For example, if poor people save their money during boom times by investing in locally available assets such as cattle or even the local stock market, these are precisely the assets that will lose their value at the same time as their businesses are hit by a drought or economic downturn. There are few savings vehicles available that are not vulnerable to the same risks as the business itself. And, in the absence of an efficient insurance market, efforts to self-insure by sharing risks with one's neighbours are subject to the same problem. The neighbours will probably be hit by a flood or a downturn at the same time as you, and there is no mechanism for sharing risk with the people on the other side of the country whose risks are not correlated with your own.

Development economists are starting to become interested in micro-savings and micro-insurance schemes to supplement the proliferation of micro-credit. They recognise that, if poor people are unable to save or insure against risk, they will tend to stick with low-risk, low-return activities which create little value for themselves or the economy.

Once again, we do not recommend that multinationals rush into micro-savings or micro-insurance, as they are likely to be as labour-intensive and unscalable as micro-credit. But we do say that, if you seek to develop local suppliers, distributors or customers, you will need to be more tolerant of their risk concerns than you would be in the developed world. Long-term contracts that shift business risk from the poor person to you make sound economic sense as the risk is then dealt with by the party most able to insure against it. The implicit insurance contained in long-term contracts creates value that can be shared between you and your local partner. Again we are facing the reality that if you are not willing to deal with these issues and offer a fair contract, you'll end up getting no contract at all.

A blast from the past

We were very proud of thinking all this through for ourselves, even if we did steal half of the basic analysis from our old tutors, Stefan Dercon and Marcel Fafchamps at Oxford University. But, sadly, we then realised it's all been said before by a greater thinker even than us—Thomas Hobbes.

> "If two people are going to co-operate, then each has to trust the other to do her bit of the work. But how can such trust build? It is possible that if the two people had worked together before, then they could trust each other on the basis of their past experience, but that can't account for the first time they worked together. It is possible that certain people—family, friends—might be able to trust each other without prior experience, but these only account for a tiny number of the actual examples that we see around us.
>
> Hobbes' answer to the dilemma was that some sort of sanction had to be available for defaulters. Those who betrayed a trust should receive some punishment (not necessarily a formal punishment—it could be a social sanction such as ostracism). One way for this to happen would be for the aggrieved party to carry out the punishment herself. But such a scheme would mean that, although the stronger party could plant one on the weaker one, the weaker would be correspondingly powerless, and so it could not work; true co-operation requires sanctions to be reciprocal, available to both parties."
>
> Source: Kieron O'Hara, *Trust . . . From Socrates to Spin* (London: Icon Books, 2004).

Hobbes was interested in how co-operation could occur in the absence of a state that could impose the rule of law. This is essentially the problem for multinationals operating in developing countries; there is rarely an effective system of law—national or international—that can control their relationships with local people. This may appear to be a strength, but is actually a weakness; as Hobbes identified, it is no use being strong if the weak then fear to deal with you.

This is why business law in many developed countries gives companies not only the right to sue but the right to *be sued*; it gives companies the crucial ability to make credible promises that they will not abuse their strength. Hobbes recommended a strong state, the Leviathan, to achieve all this in the interests of both strong and weak. In the absence of such a thing in many developing countries, clever companies need to find mechanisms to temper their own position and strengthen the relative position of their suppliers, distributors or customers. These mechanisms may take the form of publicly committing oneself to honest local dealing, writing innovative contracts that accept the local partner's overwhelming need to control risk, or clubbing together with other organisations and following a clear set of rules. All this may sound perverse, but it's soundly rooted in philosophy, economics, business strategy and game theory. The only alternative is to overpay your fellow strongmen in other international companies and the local elite.

Follow-up questions

Do your customers or suppliers need credit, insurance, information, collateral, a track record or social ties to be able to deal with you? How could you make these things available to potential customers or suppliers who don't currently have them? How could you adjust your systems to make these factors less important?

What messages could you send to potential suppliers and employees to convince them to take the opportunities you offer seriously? What information or training do they need to make credible bids? Could you club together with other companies, the host government and development bodies to develop a better local supply base?

What are development agencies and other bodies doing to overcome poverty traps? Could any of these initiatives benefit your business?

How could you write contracts and commit to behaviour that would reassure potential suppliers that the risks of dealing with you are low? Could you help them to diversify their customer base?

Further reading

'Strategies that Fit Emerging Markets' by Tarun Khanna, Krishna Palepu and Jayant Sinha, in the June 2005 issue of *Harvard Business Review*, provides an excellent account of how companies need to understand and adapt to 'institutional voids' in developing counties either by changing their business model or by helping the country to fill the gap. It is written purely from a strategy perspective rather than a poverty alleviation point of view, but reaches conclusions similar to ours. As of March 2006, you can pay to download a copy of the article from http://harvardbusinessonline.hbsp.harvard.edu.

The Mystery of Capital: Why Capitalism Triumphs in the West and Fails Everywhere Else by Hernando de Soto (published in hardback in the USA by Basic Books in 2000 and in paperback in the UK by Black Swan in 2001) is a magnificent exploration of how one poverty trap—the inability of the poor to prove collateral and gain credit—can constrain development.

Opportunity International (www.opportunity.org.uk) is a major microfinance operation and its website includes a discussion of corporate partnerships.

For links to these resources and other relevant material, go to www.makepovertybusiness.com.

Security and the poor

Poor people suffer most from insecurity

" Poor people suffer disproportionately from insecurity. They are often the worst affected by direct forms of violence, including violent crime, sexual violence and violations by local police and security personnel . . .

New kinds of security threats also take their toll. International terrorism, for example, affects poor countries directly. Casualties from international terrorism between 1998 and 2004 in Africa and Asia totalled nearly 28,000 people, compared with 5,000 people in North American and Western Europe combined. Terrorist attacks also critically damage economies. The effect of the Bali bombings was to reduce Indonesia's economic output by as much as 0.5% of GDP. The World Bank estimates that as a result of the 11 September terrorist attacks in the United States, global GDP was reduced by 0.8%, and some 10 million additional people were left in poverty as a result . . . "

Poverty increases the risks of insecurity

" Poor countries are most at risk of violent conflict . . . All other things being equal, a country at $250 GDP per capita has an average 15% chance of experiencing a civil war in the next 5 years. At a GDP per capita of $5000, the risk of civil war is less than 1%."

Source: UK Department for International Development (DFID), *Fighting Poverty to Build a Safer World: A Strategy for Security and Development* (London: DFID, March 2005; www.dfid.gov.uk/pubs/files/securityforall.pdf, 16 March 2006).

Development agencies are getting into security. Much of the impetus for this came from Clare Short, the former UK development minister, as she attempted (at times seemingly single-handedly) to rebuild Sierra Leone after the disastrous civil war there. She made the startling realisation that you can't do much economic development in a country that's wallowing in anarchy. So she instigated a widespread programme of assistance to the military, police and security services in Sierra Leone in the hope that they would not only stop organising coups and counter-coups, but also that they could make a positive contribution to stabilising the country. Stability and security are now seen by most development experts as prerequisites for investment and economic growth, although some development agencies still baulk at the type of direct support to security agencies that the UK government has pioneered.

In addition to its role in underpinning economic development, security is also increasingly seen as an end in itself. When the World Bank took the trouble to ask poor people what they wanted from development, the resulting report[23] emphasised that poor people worry just as much about crime, abuse by the security authorities, and war as they do about low incomes. Amartya Sen's view of 'development as freedom' as discussed in Chapter 3 would also measure poverty not just as income but would also include:

- Freedom from premature death in war
- Freedom from intimidation by security forces, rebel groups or gangsters
- Freedom to trade, save, farm and build without the proceeds being stolen or destroyed

Some academics have started talking about these issues as 'human security' in order to distinguish them from the 'national security' questions that have traditionally been the concern of security forces in developing coun-

23 World Bank, *Voices of the Poor: Can Anyone Hear Us?* (New York: Oxford University Press for the World Bank, 1999; www1.worldbank.org/prem/poverty/voices/reports. htm, 20 March 2006).

tries and which have often amounted to little more than keeping the current regime in power.

The fact that all of this seems rather obvious does not mean that development agencies are any good at doing it. They acknowledge, in theory, that security forces should no longer be seen as sinister, dangerous organisations that waste government money which would be better spent on health or education. They accept that security forces should be treated as public services which, just like health and education, deserve development assistance to ensure that they are effective and accountable. But, perhaps for cultural reasons, they have huge trouble dealing with security people in practice and the record of 'security-sector reform' programmes (as the jargon has it) is patchy at best.

What this means is that there is huge potential for business to:

- Influence how the security-sector reform agenda develops

- Secure development support for those business initiatives that contribute to stability and human security.

After the difficulties experienced in Afghanistan and Iraq, donors are also trying to get better at post-conflict reconstruction. The UK government has formed a cross-departmental team, the Post-Conflict Reconstruction Unit, to leap into action whenever the opportunity arises. Donors are beginning to recognise that there is a 'one-shot' opportunity to intervene at the end of a conflict, if you can use the military and related institutions to stabilise the situation but also to get essential services running, establish decent governance and kick-start economic activity. In the past, economic reform and investment promotion activities have tended to come several years after the initial military intervention, by which time hope has been lost, the cycle of conflict has restarted and international attention has moved elsewhere.

So the World Bank and other donors are keen to understand how to create the right legal, political and economic fundamentals to rapidly attract foreign investment in support of stabilisation. Again there is a huge window of opportunity for companies to ensure that their concerns are dealt with by donors and to secure maximum support for their moves into new markets.

Securing the business environment

> Companies have a duty of care to keep their employees safe and secure, and this is as true in emerging markets as it is in the UK. Their responsibilities are enshrined in law, are non-delegable, companies cannot contract out of them, and they are extra-territorial . . .
>
> The way in which a company organises its security, as well as the way it behaves more broadly within the local communities in which it operates, will ultimately impact on its continued need for security into the long-term.
>
> *Source:* Rachel Briggs, Foreign Policy Centre, 'Keeping Your People Safe: The Legal and Policy Framework for Duty of Care' (May 2003); available at fpc.org.uk/fsblob/126.pdf.

Companies have significant legal, operational and strategic reasons to be interested in security. Most immediately, they need to secure the safety of their staff and premises and, to achieve this, they often need to stabilise conditions in the local community. But, more generally, it is strongly in most companies' interests to operate in a stable, peaceful environment which:

- Allows business to be carried out predictably and safely
- Fosters economic growth and prosperity
- Does not create enormous deadweight costs in insurance premiums and physical security

Finally, a company that develops a reputation for positively influencing the security situation in a region will be welcomed into new markets by governments and donors who recognise the essential role of security in development but struggle to know how to deliver it.

The immediate challenge of keeping the company's staff and premises safe can be supported by the measures we discuss in the rest of the book such as buying as many supplies and services as possible from local companies and individuals. If local communities feel that they are benefiting from the presence of an international company, they will have less incentive to attack you and more incentive to protect you from extremists or criminals. There is nothing new about this—the military call it 'hearts and minds' and have been trying to get it right for decades. The military also make a useful distinction between 'defending' a location, which is essentially a static territorial view of holding land with guns and fences, and 'securing' a location which takes a dynamic approach to solving the underlying causes of insecurity.

The BP-led coalition that is building the Baku–Tbilisi–Ceyhan oil pipeline from Azerbaijan to Turkey recognises this issue and has contracted development organisations to implement community development programmes in every single village on the route of the pipeline. Perhaps more importantly, in keeping with our emphasis on core business activities rather than development sidelines, it has sought to implement its own security activity in ways that benefit rather than exclude the local community.

" The co-operation of local communities, as stakeholders in these projects, is critical to security. This will be achieved by working with social impact specialists, NGOs, local community leaders and local people to understand community issues and work to minimise impacts and maximise community benefits. Local security guards will be hired wherever possible. The security of the community, the most basic of human rights, will be recognised as being of equal importance as the security of those working on the project. We will work with the community to ensure this. The projects will record and report human rights allegations from the community and influence as much as possible the ethical behaviour of local forces. "

Source: Security plan for the Baku–Tbilisi–Ceyhan pipeline
(www.bp.com/genericarticle.do?categoryId=9006618&contentId=7013947).

Much of this is about style as well as substance. Can your security patrols be persuaded to take their shades off just for once and swagger a bit less? Can your security infrastructure be designed in a way that brings security to the local village as well as the factory? Are your security personnel local people who can tap into local support and tactical intelligence?

There are numerous security consultancies, often run by former military people, that can help you with these sorts of issues, and the most sophisticated ones are alive to the importance of community relations and local development rather than just providing fences, dogs and retired squaddies in tight black polo shirts. It is sometimes fashionable to dismiss the 'military' approach to security, but in fact high-level military thinking is all about having clear objectives and changing and controlling the environment in order to achieve them (rather than just sitting back and accepting chaos as inevitable 'political risk'). The case study below, written for us by a former brigadier in the British Army who now advises an international oil company, captures the discipline, sense of purpose and clarity of thinking that a military-style campaign plan can bring to the problem of security for a company. It might also indicate that there is nothing touchy-feely or wet about being concerned by poverty. The Brigadier tells me that, when you first talk about development to a tough oil man, the sceptical reply tends to be 'how many barrels of oil will that dig up?' His characteristically robust reply is: 'How many barrels of oil did you dig up in the year when you couldn't operate?'

Case study: changing the game in the Niger Delta

One of the global oil companies working in the volatile Niger Delta has started to apply military strategic campaigning techniques to help create a secure business environment.

Background. The company's operating area in the Delta straddles three ethnic groups who jockey for access to oil-related jobs and benefits, resulting in occasional armed clashes between them and, in 2003, the occupation of the company's main operating terminal in the Niger swamp. This resulted in the loss of production for over a year, and substantial damage and theft from installations in what became a virtual no-go zone.

The local communities were dominated by criminal gangs who used the freedom of a police- and military-free zone to engage in large-scale oil theft, protected by patronage from influential individuals in the public sector. The oil companies were routinely sent threats presented with a veneer of legality concerning 'taxation agreements', land ownership, rights of passage and environmental damage claims to which they responded with cash payments to buy temporary stability.

Scheme of manoeuvre. The company decided to 'change the game'. It refused to pay any further extortion and held its nerve for a year in the face of serious threats and attempted disruption by creating an alternative community development strategy. It engaged both federal and state governments using its substantial business and international influence, thereby gaining a degree of leverage at federal government level where there was a wish to restore the rule of law in the Niger Delta. The company added value to federal and state efforts by being completely transparent with UK and US development agencies over its plans for sustainable community development to achieve common goals in the Delta. It was also selective over the people it engaged with in government. Its intelligence benefited from professional procedures and absolute transparency.

Objective. The company recognised that a long-term goal was to isolate the criminal elements from the communities in the Delta. Its contribution was to create an alternative 'market' that was profitable, sustainable and attractive. The company could not afford to be too closely aligned with government security operations and that alone was no solution—there had to be a twin-track approach of security and development.

Community development partnerships. A community development programme was designed by the company including micro-business credits and partnerships with communities and government agencies to create alternative employment, business and markets. Underpinning these several campaign plans was a media information plan which used a range of psychological-operations-style messages, trusted paths and feedback mechanisms to monitor the effect of the company's activities.

Situational awareness. The management of these new initiatives proved an internal challenge to the oil company. One of the more effective tools employed was a digitisation system, which collected data and information from sensors and platforms concerning oil flows, asset movements, security and intelligence information, operational intentions and environmental issues. The data and information was collated, fused, presented graphically and flagged up to decision-makers for action.

Outcome. Two years later, the company is beginning to dictate its own terms in the Niger Delta for the self-evident benefit of everyone there. The security forces are providing a restrained presence, oil production is starting again, the community threats are diminishing and there is increasing employment. An unsuccessful attempt to occupy the company's key facility in the Delta early in 2005 was anticipated and dealt with by the State Governor in person, and the communities are slowly taking up the project opportunities that are becoming available.

The company recognised that it could not tackle this complex, long-term problem alone just as a solution had eluded both state and federal governments to date. The company recognises that this is a 10–15-year effort, but one that is essential to its own long-term business goals in the region. It is also sufficiently sanguine to anticipate changes of key people and conditions by manoeuvring quietly in advance and gaining buy-in to its intent. In the process, it is building a reputation for trust, governance and delivery and, by default, it is becoming the preferred partner of choice for all regional stakeholders.

Conclusion. In this case, we can conclude that the creation of a secure operating environment must involve the private sector where they are the major employers and the source of government revenue. More generally, it follows that private companies can play a major part in security-sector reform by creating the conditions of employment and sustainable development that erode the drift to criminality and lawlessness among communities on the edge of extreme poverty. They can be successful only if they are transparent, efficient and robust in their own operations and these are not immediately obvious profit-making schemes. It also requires a board with a long-term vision to ride the short-term costs and risks.

The benefits of success offer clear commercial advantage. The military disciplines of strategic planning and effects-based campaigning supported by good intelligence and underpinned by clear objectives and consistent leadership provide the glue of a common doctrine and process to the many different stakeholders and agendas at work. Where the private sector must not dabble is in the security regime itself—that is probably fatal to a company's long-term reputation.

As we discuss in Chapter 2, not everybody will be content with this sort of approach and will get nervous about companies being involved in development and politics. Companies don't have a good track record in managing development programmes and, if a company is going to get into this sort of activity, then it needs to be confident that it knows what it is doing and will actually create some sustainable long-term change rather than merely short-term PR benefits. Pursuing 'hearts and minds' by opening a medical clinic today and closing it next month when business priorities change is worse than useless in development terms.

What is different about the approach outlined above is that the company was not using 'community development' as a politically correct form of corruption which strengthens the status quo. As outlined in Chapter 2 on the business role in development, too often CSR and social development funds are used as a proxy for bribery in order to channel funds to the local chief by getting his cousin to build a school hall or by responding to bogus claims for environmental damage. Of course, all this does is reinforce the mind-set, power structures, dependencies and ways of working that create the problems of insecurity and under-development in the first place. Instead, this company recognises that it is in its interests to genuinely change the environment it works in. It aims to foster the rule of law and local markets that will underpin much wider development rather than just a few school halls with a corporate logo attached, and it behaves in a way that exemplifies respect for law and transparency.

The company also recognises that it has not been elected and should not interfere in politics; it co-operates with local and national government structures in ways that are consistent with its values and interests, but it does not aim to usurp the role of government or to interfere in the political process.

Assisting the government to deliver legitimate security

Through security-sector reform and other programmes, development agencies aim to help the host country deliver effective and legitimate security. Companies can usefully contribute to such efforts and, while it is certainly not the job of companies to become policemen or military officers, they can influence both the effectiveness and legitimacy of the security forces and in doing so enhance the security of their own operations.

Companies can contribute to effectiveness by providing mentoring, infrastructure and advice to security agencies. In South Africa, the 'Business Against Crime' initiative has brought together a coalition of businesses to support the South African police force. They are particularly active in the province of Gauteng, the industrial and business heartland of South Africa which includes the cities of Pretoria and Johannesburg and which suffers high levels of crime even by the standards of South Africa. Programmes include:

- Installing closed-circuit television (CCTV) in Johannesburg's central business district
- Providing mentoring for 53 police stations in the province
- Supporting a Victim Support Programme in 45 police stations
- Supporting management training for police officers at South African universities
- Supporting education in 400 schools

The collective benefits for a group of businesses to reduce crime in their operating areas are clear and range from reduced insurance premiums through to the efficiency gains of sharing the costs of security rather than making expensive individual provision—there's little point in each business putting their own CCTV camera on a lamppost when they could all share the costs of putting up just one.

But, if we are being rigorous about the business case, we have to consider the economic old chestnut of the 'free-riding problem'—why not let everyone else fund the programme and just reap the benefits, because less crime in your city will benefit you whether or not you're a member of the scheme? Of course, the problem with this attitude is that, if everyone thinks the same, then no one will join in and the collective action won't happen at all.

The classic theoretical case of this free-rider problem is the lighthouse—as a ship owner you get the benefits of a lighthouse whether or not you've contributed to the cost of its construction. For years, many economists said that lighthouses could only be provided by the government, and, if the government weren't able or willing to do the job, then they just wouldn't be built. But this was confounded by the historical facts—private entrepreneurs did make money by building lighthouses. They did so by linking lighthouses to nearby ports; you could charge ship owners for access to ports and you could use some of that money to pay for the lighthouse. Thus shipowners paid for a bundle of benefits which included port access (where access could be controlled and so payment could be made compulsory) and the benefits of a nearby lighthouse.

Now this is the sort of thing that Nobel Prize winners argue about and we fear we're already getting lost in too much detail. But the important thing for us is to note that collective action on crime does take place, just as private lighthouses did exist, regardless of what the theory says, and our job is to explain how we can achieve similar results elsewhere. It seems very likely that, just as in the lighthouse case, when a company pays for a public benefit such as crime control, it also gets some private benefits. The private benefits of joining the crime control club might include access to business opportunities from being part of an influential network of business people and politicians (or, more accurately, avoiding the danger of being ostracised by them if you do not chip in). You also gain the opportunity to influence police priorities and to gain intelligence and understanding which you can use to guide your own security activity.

Of course there is a risk to these types of activities. You do not want to make a police or security force more efficient if that just means it can crack more heads, repress more people and better prop up a disgraceful regime. The security force has to be have some degree of legitimacy with the people and be responding to their concerns rather than simply enforcing the will of an undemocratic regime or one small subset of society. But this takes us into deeply into sensitive political issues and it would be a foolish company that started campaigning against the practices of the host government and its security agencies. Wouldn't it be better to leave well alone?

The good news is that, in some countries, there may be activities that can make a security force more legitimate without the need to campaign for wholesale political change. The security-sector reform agenda places great emphasis on Security Sector Reviews, which are designed to underpin the reform process by going back to first principles:

- What are the main security concerns of the people?
- What are the ambitions of the people for development and freedom, and what threatens to undermine them?
- What threats do the security forces need to counter?
- What resources do they need to do so?
- How does security activity support wider development?

The aim is to ensure that the activities of the police and security forces are aligned with the needs of the people for human security, rather than simply defending the ruling class or lined up against an imagined foreign enemy in order to justify huge military expenditure.

For example, in Sierra Leone, the Office of National Security conducted a Security Sector Review by carrying out an unprecedented consultation with a huge cross-section of grassroots opinion. It learned that most people's main concerns were issues such as corruption and bad governance rather than the threat from neighbouring countries that senior security officials spent most of their time worrying about. The result was a significant realignment of activity and the inclusion of security in Sierra Leone's Poverty Reduction Strategy Paper to underline the links between security and development and to ensure that the security sector received proper resources and support from donors. The important point to make is that many security officials welcomed the review as it put them on a legitimate footing, guaranteed them international co-operation, and helped them to secure the support of the people for their operations.

Companies can play a role in facilitating this sort of process—the important element being that they are neutrally helping all parties to express an opinion rather than taking sides. Of course, there are some countries where even this sort of minor consultation would be anathema to an authoritarian government. But there are plenty more that are moving tentatively towards security-sector reform in order to support economic development and secure international approval. We have been involved in such processes in places as diverse as Guatemala, Kosovo and Indonesia. It would have been extremely useful to have been able to consult a collective of companies that could represent private-sector concerns, organise consultations with employees and tease out the links between insecurity and lack of economic growth.

The Confederation of British Industry (CBI) played this sort of role in the 1990s in Northern Ireland. In 1994, it published a peace dividend paper that outlined all the problems of high security costs, lack of investment and brain drain that instability caused in Northern Ireland, and it also emphasised all the economic opportunities that could be found if the troubles ceased. The CBI later joined up with six other employer and trade union groups and used their collective authority to make the business case for peace, organise dialogue between the political parties, and maintain the momentum for peace in the media and in public opinion. They were impartial throughout and wielded their authority only when the normal political mechanisms were failing and some outside impetus was required.

This is, inevitably, a political minefield and not one that companies will wish to enter alone. But, if you can form a group of companies with similar security concerns and link up with donor or government activity in the field, you could ensure that your security needs, and those of your employees and community, are more efficiently and legitimately met by government.

Contributing to national stability and post-conflict reconstruction

●●Most of the larger international companies now emphasize the importance of corporate social responsibility and this often includes charitable endeavours such as corporate sponsorships of education or health programmes. Such initiatives are important in their own right, but companies' most significant social impact will come from the way that they conduct their core activities, and in particular from the relationships with local communities and sub-contractors. **"**

Source: John Bray, *International Companies and Post-Conflict Reconstruction* (Working Paper 22; Washington, DC: World Bank Conflict Prevention and Reconstruction Unit, February 2005; http://rru.worldbank.org/PapersLinks/Conflict-Affected-Countries, 20 March 2006).

All of the economic development in the world and all of the business efforts to secure the local environment will mean nothing if the entire country falls into civil war or fails to escape from a cycle of conflict. Businesses therefore need to consider how their operations can increase or decrease the risk of major instability. The most basic principle should be to 'do no wrong', but there are also a host of positive things a company can do to lessen the prospect of conflict in their host countries.

It is common to think of conflict as something inevitable in the human condition, based on long-standing hatreds and complex religious and ethnic rivalries, the details of which are lost in time and inexplicable to the outsider. If we took this view, then it is difficult to see how an international company could influence conflict for good *or* bad. But the evidence shows something quite different. The Oxford economist Professor Paul Collier writes as follows:

> The discourse on conflict tends to be dominated by group griev-
> ances beneath which inter-group hatreds lurk, often traced back
> through history. I have investigated statistically the global pat-
> tern of large-scale civil conflict since 1965, expecting to find a close
> relationship between measures of these hatreds and grievances
> and the incidence of conflict. Instead, I found that economic
> agendas appear to be central to understanding why civil wars get
> going. Conflicts are far more likely to be caused by economic *oppor-
> tunities* [our emphasis] than by grievance.[24]

We are back to our central theme that what matters is not only economic growth and a thriving business sector, but the precise *nature* of the activity. The opening-up of economic opportunity can be counterproductive if it creates competition between groups over who gets the spoils. This is the reason that many development people talk about the 'resource curse'—the counter-intuitive idea that countries develop more strongly over the long

24 Paul Collier, The World Bank, 'Doing Well out of War' (10 April 1999); available at www.worldbank.org/research/conflict/papers/econagendas.pdf.

term if they do *not* have valuable natural resources. The logic behind this is that in a country where the government controls valuable resources, not only will clever people spend their time trying to control government rather than creating new value in business and entrepreneurship, but there will also be conflict among the different groups who are all fighting to get a piece of the same pie.

Of course, natural resources are not the only thing that can cause a violent or wasteful struggle for political power and crowd out honest entrepreneurship. Badly directed development money and increased opportunities for demanding bribes from business both create disproportionate incentives for people to try to gain control of government and communities. (When we look around development conferences at all the clever local people from NGOs and government competing for development grants and CSR projects, we often wonder whether we'd all be better off if they used their talents to start a tyre repair shop or taxi service.)

In this context, a business has to consider whether its activities are exacerbating or reducing the battle between different groups for money and power. The academic Mary Anderson refers to 'connectors' and 'dividers'. Connectors are organisations or projects that bring people together through a shared interest in a common objective, e.g. the construction of a road that benefits all communities or a business that creates opportunities for all. Dividers reinforce social fragmentation by encouraging a winner-takes-all attitude to development. If your company creates more opportunities for the Prime Minister to get rich through corruption than it does for local entrepreneurs, or if your CSR activities give most money to the most vocal communities at the expense of everyone else, then you're probably a divider.

Throughout this book, we suggest ways in which the benefits of your presence can be spread as widely as possible and, in particular, how you can include groups that have not traditionally benefited from economic opportunity. There is a clear business case for doing so—one of the most influential ideas in business strategy, Michael Porter's famous Five Forces,[25] is that you want to maximise your number of potential suppliers and customers. But, in addition to the strong business case, you may also be having a fundamental impact on stability and ultimately poverty by reducing the conflict between different groups.

Where perhaps we differ from the more optimistic authors (see the box below) about the positive role of business is that companies do not auto-

---

25 Michael Porter, 'How Competitive Forces Shape Strategy', *Harvard Business Review*, 1 March 1979; or see en.wikipedia.org/wiki/Porter_5_forces_analysis for an overview.

matically do the optimal thing, even when the business case is pretty clear. It is easy to fall into the traps of dealing with only one ethnic group or buying only from fellow international companies and, in the short term, these traps have their own powerful logic. We discussed this further in Chapter 4 on poverty/inefficiency traps. The stabilising effects of business come only when managers understand the pitfalls and work hard, sometimes at short-term risk and cost, to overcome them.

One of the characteristics of conflict economics is that rival protagonists tend to see development as a zero sum game. In a divided society—for example post-war Bosnia-Herzegovina—one community's commercial gain is often seen as a loss to its rivals. Business planners tend to see things differently. Bosnia-Herzegovina is in any case a small market, and social divisions risk making it even smaller—they need as many customers as possible and look for the best employees, regardless of their ethnic origin. The logic of ethnic politics and the war economy is divisive—the logic of a more open economy is inclusive.

By presenting a vision of a different kind of future, where personal success comes from entrepreneurial initiative rather than military expertise, international companies and their local partners can help find a way out of cycles of deprivation and conflict. In the worst cases, companies can inadvertently fuel the structural causes of conflict, undermining prospects for recovery. In the best case, their most important contributions may not be money, nor even expertise, but hope.

Source: John Bray, *International Companies and Post-Conflict Reconstruction* (Working Paper 22; Washington, DC: World Bank Conflict Prevention and Reconstruction Unit, February 2005; http://rru.worldbank.org/PapersLinks/Conflict-Affected-Countries/, 20 March 2006).

Follow-up questions

Are your security operations involving or alienating your local community? How could you work together to deliver mutual security?

Are there elements of your security operations that could be delivered more cheaply and effectively if you clubbed together with other businesses?

What private benefits in the form of influence, information, networking or reputation could be attached to club membership?

What could you do to support the government's need to deliver legitimate security? How can you help them understand the security needs of business and the community?

Are your business and CSR activities reinforcing or undermining the sources of conflict and instability? How could you make honest entrepreneurship more profitable than grabs for local or national political power?

Further reading

The Business of Peace: The Private Sector as a Partner in Conflict Prevention and Resolution by Jane Nelson, published in London by International Alert, the Council on Economic Priorities and The Prince of Wales Business Leaders Forum in 2000 gives an excellent systematic account of the positive and negative ways in which companies can affect security, broken down by the type of business operation and the type of conflict you find yourself in. It includes several case histories. It is difficult to find but as, of March 2006, was available from Amazon with a few weeks' delay.

Joining Forces: From National Security to Networked Security by Rachel Briggs, published by the London-based think-tank Demos in 2005, looks mostly at security in the UK, but makes some useful general points about the need for government to co-operate with business in providing security. As of March 2006, the book was available for free download at www.demos.co.uk/catalogue/joiningforcesbook where you can also purchase a hard copy. The book is part of a long-term project to examine the business case for working on security and to outline business's role in security-sector reform. Further reports from the project are expected to be published throughout 2006 and will be available at www.demos.co.uk.

The Peace Dividend Trust (www.peacedividendtrust.org) does interesting work to increase the level of backward linkages between UN peacekeeping operations and the local economy, with the aim of contributing to local development and stability. Their website includes a useful paper which contains many recommendations that could also be adopted by businesses operating in post-conflict countries.

For links to these resources and other relevant material, go to www.makepovertybusiness.com.

Partnering and co-operating to reduce poverty

6

> Companies in diverse sectors around the world face increasingly complex risks and opportunities for shareholder value and project success linked to social and environmental issues. Partnerships with civil society and public sector agencies can be a highly efficient way to manage these challenges successfully and thrive in business terms.

Source: Rob Lake, Head of Engagement and Corporate Governance, Henderson Global Investors (quoted in *Putting Partnering to Work*, cited below).

> We work with other companies, especially local suppliers and contractors. And we work with NGOs and governments . . . In Colombia we couldn't have made progress in assisting the communities of Casanare without the active help of agencies such as CARE International and the World Bank, but also, and most important, from the help of local authorities and local NGOs.

Source: Lord Browne, BP Group Chief Executive, February 2002 (quoted in *Putting Partnering to Work*, cited below).

●● Tri-sector partnerships [partnerships with governments and NGOs] enable the company to focus on those aspects of community development it is best placed to deliver, for example, clearing supplies through customs, 'rolling out' operational infrastructure to communities, extending employment and procurement opportunities, seconding skilled staff and loaning heavy equipment. This is particularly important in the current context, where the approaches of companies to social investment often tend to be a duplication of the activities of NGOs, local government, donor agencies, or community-based organisations, rather than contributing what is unique about the presence of a private sector operation. ●●

Source: Business Partners for Development (BPD), *Putting Partnering to Work: Tri-sector Partnership Results and Recommendations for Businesses* (London: BPD, 2002; www.bpdweb.com/docs/biz4of5.pdf, 20 March 2006).

In Chapter 2, we talked about some of the pitfalls for companies that find themselves directly involved in development and, in particular, the dangers of trying to implement projects when you don't have the competencies or incentives to do them properly. One of the obvious ways to overcome this problem is by partnering or co-operating with local organisations that can supplement your business skills with experience in economic and development issues plus local knowledge and connections.

Much of the work in this field has focused on how partnerships can be formed in order to implement a development project unconnected to the core business. The incentives for a business to be involved in such work tend to be based on corporate social responsibility or 'licence to operate' arguments: for example, when implementing community initiatives around a major oil or mining project. These partnerships and projects may be essential for maintaining reputation or creating a secure environment, but they do not draw on many of the company's real skills and what looks like a partnership may in fact be a simple question of outsourcing social responsibilities to an NGO. There is nothing wrong in this development partnership approach and, given our concerns about companies attempting ill-informed and unco-ordinated development on their own, then outsourcing should be welcomed. But as our main interest is in using the core business we will not spend much time on it here.

Of more interest is the case when companies want to extend their business to areas or people that may not be currently profitable and need the help of a non-profit organisation to achieve it.

There are several reasons why a company might want to partner with a non-profit organisation to serve a non-profitable sector. In some cases, unprofitable activities are an explicit part of a government contract; for example, water supply contracts for cities often include a coverage provision that forces companies to supply both rich and poor areas and, in effect, part of the profit from the rich areas is used to cross-subsidise operations for the poor. In other cases, there is no explicit contractual condition but companies feel they are more likely to win contracts or secure licences if they can guarantee widespread service provision. Sometimes companies may want to benefit from a non-profit organisation's contacts, experience and influence in order to carry out their main business, and so have to demonstrate that part of their proposal has development benefit and could not be achieved by the profit motive alone.

The case of Telenor in Bangladesh captures many of these points.[26] Telenor, the Norwegian telecommunications company, was approached by the famous micro-finance organisation Grameen Bank, and encouraged to supply mobile phone services to the poor of Bangladesh. Grameen is a strictly non-profit organisation, which is 93% owned by its borrowers with the remainder owned by the Government of Bangladesh. It had extended credit to Bangladesh's poor through a network of village self-help groups and now wanted to use the same community understanding and network of contacts to provide villages with links to the outside world.

Telenor assessed that there were two distinct markets in Bangladesh. There was an urban market of around 5% of the population who could afford mobile services and could be profitably served through a conventional business model. Telenor aimed to be the first foreign provider to secure a licence to serve this premium market—a mere 5% of Bangladesh still added up to more than the entire population of Norway. Then there was the vast rural market which was poor, dispersed, short of collateral or credit track records, difficult to serve and wholly unfamiliar to Telenor.

Even the premium urban market would not be straightforward. There were huge country risks in investing in a country with no independent telecommunications regulator and a political and economic environment very different from that in Norway. However, Telenor saw that Grameen could be an essential partner in navigating this political and cultural labyrinth if a partnership could be formed that would meet:

26 This case study is mostly based on: P. Malaviya, E. O'Keefe and A. Ellidge, 'Creating Value for the Poor', *INSEAD Quarterly*, July–September 2005: 18-21; available at www.insead.edu/discover_INSEAD/publications/documents/IQ11.pdf.

- Telenor's needs for profits and certainty
- Grameen's needs for tangible progress on development

To meet the different parties' objectives, two vehicles were formed. Grameen Phone was a joint venture between Telenor and Grameen and some smaller partners, with Telenor holding 51% of the equity. Grameen Phone focused on providing the basic mobile infrastructure and directly serving the urban market. This urban business became hugely successful for Telenor. By 2004 it had 2.6 million subscribers with earnings before interest, tax, depreciation and amortisation (EBITDA) margins of 40–50%. Its market value was estimated at around $600 million, which was 15 times the initial Telenor investment of $40 million and four times Telenor's total cumulative investment. One financial analyst described Grameen Phone as 'a diamond in Telenor's portfolio'. Telenor has since used some of the lessons learned from the project to enter another low-income market in Pakistan.

A separate non-profit company, Grameen Telecom, wholly owned by Grameen Bank, purchased mobile services from Grameen Phone at half price, and aimed simply to cover its costs by serving the rural market through a network of 'village phone ladies'. These 'phone ladies', all existing members of Grameen Bank, would purchase a handset using a Grameen loan and rent the phone to other villagers to make calls. This created a multiplier effect in which one phone was used by many different people and it was estimated that, by placing 70,000 phones in 40,000 villages, Grameen provided mobile telephone access to millions of people.

In addition to the direct benefits to the poor as customers, Grameen Phone also became the biggest foreign investor in Bangladesh, the second biggest taxpayer and one of the country's largest employers, with all the spin-off development benefits we discuss elsewhere in the book.

This is a great example of playing to each party's different strengths and objectives in a productive partnership. Telenor could provide infrastructure and conventional service to wealthy urban customers, but had no local knowledge or influence. Grameen could fill these gaps and help Telenor to thrive in the urban market, but only if their development objectives were met by also serving the rural poor. Telenor played no role in serving the wholly unfamiliar rural market other than simply selling mobile services to Grameen, who then used its skills and networks to do the difficult job of managing rural subscribers. The basic product was the same, but was marketed and managed very differently in the two markets, and with different but complementary objectives.

There are several lessons here for forming partnerships with non-profit organisations. The first is that each side should be explicit about their over-all objectives. There is no point in pretending to have philanthropic motivations in order to get on with your new partners, only to let them down when head office starts pressuring for profits. A wise NGO will understand your need to make profits and will enter a project only if it sees a way to use that motive to further its development aims.

The second is to be clear about the strengths and weaknesses that each party is bringing to the project and to be willing to heed the other's advice. Non-profit organisations—and pressure groups in particular—are often willing to work with companies in order to exert influence and lead change, but they get very upset if they believe they are simply being used for their logos and reputation rather than because their advice is valued.

Finally, partnerships need to come together for a specific purpose rather than as ends in themselves. As in any other project, each partner needs clear goals, responsibilities and incentives.

What help can multinationals obtain from embassies?

Expatriates operating overseas can often secure advice and assistance from their home-country embassy and, occasionally, this may even go beyond securing illicit duty-free alcohol for a party. However the different ministries represented in an embassy will have different agendas and it is important to understand the policies and constraints they work under before requesting assistance. We will take the British system as our example of the sort of support that can be obtained, but many of the lessons will be applicable to other nation's embassies as well.

Ambassadors are normally drawn from the Foreign and Commonwealth Office (FCO) and will be specifically charged with supporting British commercial interests. It is part of their job to give you political and economic advice and to facilitate your dealings with the local government. For ambitious ambassadors, this area is one of their real opportunities to shine and there is nothing they like more than when your chairman tells the Prime Minister how supportive they have been. Equally, they will have a strong fear of complaints that they are not sufficiently supportive of British business.

Interestingly, the definition of what constitutes a 'British' business is far from clear, particularly in a world of widely diversified shareholders. In practice, expatriates will secure at least tacit support if:

- They personally are British

- Their company is traditionally thought of as being British

- Their company has close links to the UK

- Their company employs a significant number of British people

The Ambassador's specific role in supporting UK commercial interests will be supported by the Commercial section, but the calibre of these sections varies and they often understand little about your business. It may be more valuable, particularly as you are probably looking for political and economic advice rather than specific commercial support, to go directly to the Ambassador, the Political Counsellor or the First Secretary. They will often supply you with the sort of political gossip that most people have to pay the Economist Intelligence Unit to receive. There is rarely a systematic way of organising this sort of support and much depends on the strength of your personal relationship with the individual concerned. Do not forget that diplomats may be feeling isolated and homesick just as much as anyone else, and will often welcome dinner and party invitations from a friendly fellow Brit.

FCO staff often have access to small project funds which they will allocate to worthy causes that will also strengthen the UK's reputation in the country. It is often difficult to find decent opportunities to donate this cash and then monitor how it is spent, and they may welcome ideas and assistance.

The UK's development programme in most countries is run by officials from the Department for International Development (DFID), and it is important to understand that they have very different objectives and policies from the FCO. By law, DFID is allowed to pursue policies only in the development interests of the host government and may not take British national or commercial interests into account. This ruling is a reaction to the bad old days of 'tied aid' when projects were often chosen based on how much they propped up ailing British suppliers rather than how much they benefited the host country.

These rules against pursuing the national interest are interpreted very strictly and indeed many DFID people interpret a national interest argument as positively *undermining* a development case rather than being strictly irrelevant, as the law requires. It is therefore essential that you understand the development arguments clearly when seeking support from DFID. But, if you are able to persuade them of your goodwill, they can often be extremely supportive in:

- Explaining the host country's development priorities
- Outlining existing activity by donors and NGOs
- Making introductions

In many developing countries, DFID are major funders of the economy and the government, and so will often have better local contacts and understanding than the FCO. Even more than with the FCO, you will best secure their support by establishing a strong personal relationship as they have no duty to support you simply because you are a British company.

What help can multinationals obtain from international development agencies?

One might think that the confluence of the interest in poverty reduction of international development agencies and the poverty-reducing ability of global corporations, along with the smattering of positive examples such as the Grameen case, would lead to fulsome alliances between businesses, international development agencies and NGOs. Unfortunately—and oddly— this is not really the case and we do not see as many positive examples of joint work as we might expect. The degree of interface between relevant international development agencies such as the World Bank and the United Nations Development Programme (UNDP), along with NGOs such as Oxfam and global corporations such as Nestlé, Shell or GE is remarkably modest.

As we have suggested before, there is nothing more inimical to the interests of global corporations than poverty. A lower incidence of poverty means more and richer markets. But this most obvious of points—and the overwhelming ability of MNCs to create and store wealth—has not led to a harnessing of their abilities to help drive poverty reduction in poor countries. There are quite a few reasons for this. Principal among them is that in many quarters of development institutions and, perhaps more importantly, in many leading NGOs that hold sway over these institutions, there is a belief in an equation that big companies equal exploitation and badness, and a blind eye is turned to the creation of jobs, markets, new products, sales and exports. This is a legitimacy problem[27] that costs big business a lot of money every day and, more importantly for our world, keeps more people in poverty than there otherwise would be. Another reason is that there is a restraint in international and bilateral development agencies to partner with individual companies in case the benefits of project activities flow to individuals and private businesses rather than societies—a rather purist point which, as we've identified, ignores the many spin-off benefits of business to the wider community.

As an example of this political minefield, the UNDP attempted in 1998 to forge a form of commercial alliance with a set of big companies in order to help the poor, but this was howled down by a consortium of NGOs and they greeted their successful wrecking of this venture with glee. See the box below for details of this sorry tale.[28]

UNDP's proposal for a 'global sustainable development facility'

The proposal was initiated internally by the UNDP early in 1998. A UNDP project manager was appointed and interest was solicited from a range of major global corporations. By July 1998, 11 corporations had agreed to participate in the feasibility phase of the Global Sustainable Development Facility (GSDF). These included IKEA and Ericsson of Sweden, Rio Tinto of the UK and Australia, Citibank of the USA and Statoil of Norway. UNDP proceeded to design potential projects and appoint advisers to the project steering committee. Planning commenced for a project launch in mid-1999 following completion of the feasibility phase.

During the feasibility phase, the GSDF initiative was described by UNDP as follows: 'The Global Sustainable Development Facility project is an initiative that brings together leading global corporations and the UNDP to jointly define and implement a new facility to eradicate poverty, create sustainable economic growth, and allow the private sector to prosper through the inclusion of two billion new people in the global market economy. The first of its kind, this new initiative will bring UNDP's universality, 40 years of development experience, and network of offices in

---

27   See G.C. Lodge and C. Wilson, *A Corporate Solution to Global Poverty: How Multinationals Can Help the Poor and Invigorate Their Legitimacy* (Princeton University Press, 2006) which tackles the question of legitimacy of corporations and gives more details on the interface between international development architecture and global business.

28   *Ibid.*: 111.

developing countries together with the knowledge and resources of the private sector.'

Ultimately, the launch was aborted. The GSDF had intended to involve corporations fully and formally in major development initiatives. The GSDF had been proposed as an independent legal entity, governed and capitalised by corporate partners, operating within agreed UN development parameters. UNDP senior officials, in the face of criticism of NGO partners, shelved the GSDF proposal. The NGOs Corpwatch and Amnesty International led the charge to end the UNDP GSDF proposal and boasted of their success.

Source: interviews with various UNDP staff, a UNDP GSDF launch preparation document, and reports from www.corpwatch.org

---

So, to date, there has not been any real and systematic partnership between big business and the international development agencies in the pursuit of sustainable poverty reduction. This is despite the fact that big business and the forces of globalisation, albeit not without mistakes and negative impacts, lessen poverty more than any other single form of intervention.

Some organisations are working to remedy this shortcoming. The World Business Council for Sustainable Development in Switzerland is one and the International Business Leaders Forum in the UK is another. Such organisations, along with country-based NGOs such as Grameen, often make much more attractive implementation partners for companies as they are free from the political baggage of many international organisations and, at least, accept the basic premise that the profit motive can be harnessed for development.

The UN itself has formed the Global Compact, which nearly 2,000 corporations have now joined—but this is more an expression of intent to act as good corporate citizens than a practical way to bring MNCs into the fight against poverty. It is effectively a list of self-imposed constraints, which may be uncontroversial in themselves, but tell only half the story as they have no positive view of what business might contribute to development.

Global Compact Principles

On human rights:

- Principle 1: Businesses should support and respect the protection of internationally proclaimed human rights.

- Principle 2: Businesses should make sure that they are not complicit in human rights abuses.

On labour standards:

- Principle 3: Businesses should uphold the freedom of association and the effective recognition of the right to collective bargaining.
- Principle 4: Businesses should uphold the elimination of all forms of forced and compulsory labour.
- Principle 5: Businesses should uphold the effective abolition of child labour.
- Principle 6: Businesses should uphold the elimination of discrimination in respect of employment and occupation.

On environment:

- Principle 7: Businesses should support a precautionary approach to environmental challenges.
- Principle 8: Businesses should undertake initiatives to promote greater environmental responsibility.
- Principle 9: Businesses should encourage the development and diffusion of environmentally friendly technologies.

On anti-corruption:

- Principle 10: Businesses should work against all forms of corruption, including extortion and bribery.

Source: UN Global Compact (www.unglobalcompact.org/AboutTheGC/TheTenPrinciples/index.html, 17 March 2006).

The World Bank led a useful programme in the late 1990s, known as Business Partners for Development, which sought to capture examples of business, governments and NGOs co-operating to achieve shared development objectives. The degree of replication is not certain but this programme did help to promote the 'partnership' agenda.

In 2003, the UNDP established the Commission for Private Sector and Development, but this was more an analytical process which ended up promoting a focus on the development of small and medium-sized enterprises (SMEs), not a new concept and certainly not one without its critics. The UNDP also has a partnership project, deliberately kept small for some of the political reasons outlined above, called Global Sustainable Business for Poverty Reduction. This programme has sought, at a country level, to arrange partnerships between individual corporations and local projects, e.g. village fuel projects or primary healthcare. There are a handful of examples from this programme, mostly in Africa.

The sad truth is that, if a company wants to undertake work directly targeted at reducing poverty and measure the impacts of their effort, there is no systematic support to be had for this. In fact, as noted in Chapter 3 on the extent of poverty, mechanisms for measuring poverty impact at a micro level simply do not exist and big companies have never been encouraged to measure their impacts in poverty terms. And, in the premier system for poverty reduction at a country level, Poverty Reduction Strategy Papers (PRSPs), led by the World Bank and IMF in partnership with the host country, there is not a single word about multinational corporations—which in many countries, especially smaller ones, often single-handedly drive the economies. The PRSPs make a major point of emphasising the importance of participation and stakeholder discussion, but MNCs remain 'outside the tent'. Given their importance in reducing poverty, this is a curious and lamentable outcome. We hope that this book might help herald a change in this respect.

So we are faced with a mixed picture. Large-scale systematic efforts to link companies to international development agencies and major NGOs are often proposed but rarely enacted, partly because of the influence of anti-business NGOs. However, it may be easier to get practical small-scale help on the ground from members of international donor organisations who understand your business and development case and are frustrated by the constraints imposed by international politics. There are also a growing number of international organisations, embassies and local NGOs, unconstrained by UN politics, that are eager to help. The key to securing their support is understanding and aligning your different objectives and treating them with respect, rather than simply trying to borrow their stamp of approval for your annual report.

Follow-up questions

Could NGOs and donors help you to navigate complex political and social environments and reach new customers and suppliers? What incentives, in terms of concrete progress on development, could you offer them to work with you? Does each side understand the other's motivation, strengths and weaknesses? What clear objectives and measures could you agree?

What practical help could you secure from international organisations at the local level? At the international level, should your company be lobbying for better systematic support?

Further reading

The Business Partners for Development (BPD) project developed concrete advice for managing different types of partnership between business, government and NGOs. It has several good examples of productive partnerships, particularly in the water and extractive industries. As of March 2006, its material was available for free download from its website (www.bpdweb.com).

The Prince of Wales International Business Leaders Forum (IBLF) (www.iblf.org) offers advice and support to companies that want to do more in their local community, and will often facilitate collective action by companies and NGOs.

The World Business Council for Sustainable Development (WBCSD) (www.wbcsd.org) is a consortium of businesses interested in development and environmental issues. It also supports a network of national-level Business Councils for Sustainable Development.

For links to these resources and other relevant material, go to www.makepovertybusiness.com.

Innovation for
poverty reduction

A lot of rubbish has been written about innovation, some of it by us. During the breathless dot.com boom, companies everywhere were being exhorted to act more like entrepreneurs, to take bigger risks and to forget everything they thought they once knew. Of course, most of it turned out to be nonsense. The entrepreneurs that were held up as heroes mostly failed, and the companies that most embraced innovation have gone out of fashion. If we are to make progress on profitable poverty reduction, which is really only a special case of innovation, what lessons can we learn from the varying fortunes of the idea of innovation? How can we develop truly valuable opportunities and implement them effectively in a company without risking our own careers or the company's profits?

We do not underestimate the difficulty of all this—one of our friends has just been promoted to his first really serious job in a major multinational and been told he'll be sacked unless he meets his annual targets. It's hard for him to focus on corporate reputation or long-term profitability or, for goodness' sake, poverty reduction when his mortgage and his kids' schooling and his status in the industry depend on how much profit his small bit of the company makes over the next 12 months. He cannot act like an entrepreneur because he doesn't have the same incentives as an entrepreneur.

For our friend's benefit, we like to talk about **'conservative innovation'**. We use 'conservative' not only because it makes a nice contrast with 'innovation', but also because we specifically want to draw on the work of conservative thinkers who have analysed the proper balance between change and continuity. Our aim is to help you think through what might realistically work in your company with its specific history, skills and culture—not to give you a lot of high-risk stuff which seems to have worked for other people.

So, first of all, we'll clear the air about what we mean by innovation and what's desirable and realistic to achieve in a large company. Then we'll talk about what innovation means in the specific context of poverty reduction. What do we want to be innovative about? What's the relevance to the core business? Then we'll talk about structures and methods for achieving innovation. Finally, we'll complete the circle by discussing how innovation in developing countries can be re-adopted back into developed-country markets.

To kick things off, we'll go through a few of the 'nonsense' statements that have become accepted wisdom about innovation and then propose our own view.

Nonsense statement no. 1: entrepreneurs are better than big companies at innovation

There's a well-known stylised fact (meaning we can't remember the source) that says that around 95% of new products or services came from companies employing fewer than a hundred people. We once constructed a complex argument around this statistic to do with the idea that small companies were less hidebound by tradition and could move faster than large companies. Our business school tutor, the excellent John Weeks at INSEAD, simply replied: 'small companies invent more things than big companies because there are more small companies than big companies'.

He's right of course. When we look at any industry, we can examine the specific innovations and we'll probably find that many have been brought forward by a small company. For example, if we look at the coffee industry we might wonder why the then start-up Starbucks came up with the Starbucks concept and not, say, Nestlé. We might then conclude that (formerly) small companies like Starbucks are 'better' at innovation than large companies like Nestlé.

But this is nonsense. Starbucks may indeed be better in some ways than Nestlé, but what about Sid's Coffee Shop and Fred's Café and all the other small companies we've never heard of that didn't invent the Starbucks concept either? Are *they* better or worse than Nestlé?

The market is full of small companies and entrepreneurs all trying out a crazy variety of ideas. The vast majority fail. Occasionally one of them comes up with something brilliant and we use this as evidence that small companies are good at innovation. The failures fail quietly and we never hear of them again. In the trade, this is known as survivor bias—by definition, we only know about and study the successful entrepreneurs because the unsuccessful ones disappear. In contrast, there are a small number of big companies whose every move is scrutinised by the market. We're able to study their every success and every failure, and we're far more intolerant of their cock-ups and oversights than we are of all the small companies who didn't make it to the big innovation either.

Nonsense statement no. 2: big companies should act more like entrepreneurs

Our second stylised fact, related to the first and a commonplace of industrial organisation theory, is that small companies have a high failure rate but those that do survive grow rapidly. In contrast, large companies have a low failure rate but they all grow slowly. There's a sense that large companies get things just about right and that small companies mostly get things wrong but, when they get things right, they get them exactly right.

Entrepreneurs have the huge luxury that they can fail quietly and move on to their next experiment. Corporations, and the executives within them, have no such freedom and have to be more risk-averse. Innovation advocates won't like this, but there's nothing inherently wrong with this state of affairs. As a shareholder I choose what type of risk and return I want. If I invest in 'Boring PLC' then it's for a good reason and I don't want them to suddenly turn into 'ponytailedgit.com', no matter how bored their executives get.

The chief executive of Royal Dutch/Shell group, Jeroen van der Veer, makes a useful analogy when explaining Shell's famous use of scenario planning. He argues that, when an entrepreneur faces two possible scenarios of 'rain' or 'sun', he tends to choose to stock either umbrellas or ice cream. The entrepreneur who gets it right will make a fortune and the one who gets it wrong will get nothing. Shell, as a large company with risk-averse investors, could stock both umbrellas and ice cream but that would be expensive and inefficient. Instead they always search for the 'chocolate bar'—the thing that will work in either outcome. The result is lower risk but will always be less lucrative than making (the right!) distinctive, high-risk choice.

Nonsense statement no. 3: big companies are 'constrained' by their history and structure

Why do large companies have a far higher survival rate than small companies? Well, first of all they've become big because they've hit upon something that works. They've had time to perfect their products, services and working methods in the market and have finally found an effective mixture. And, when they try something new, they can easily test it with their network of experienced management, experts, customers, suppliers and advisers before investing too much time and money. In contrast, an entrepreneur, 'unconstrained' by history or an existing structure, has to set up a company, open a bank account, persuade someone to build a prototype, get some marketing advice, etc. etc. ad nauseam before being able to go to market. If you're from Unilever and you've got a great idea, then you can be sure that some serious bankers and advertisers will rally round to talk to you about it—but try getting that sort of advice when you're phoning from your entrepreneurial garage. No wonder so many entrepreneurs fail. They have to spend all their money just getting together the bare bones of a business before they can test anything with experts or in the market.

The economist Richard Nelson puts it like this:

> [An institution] is like a paved road across a swamp. To say the
> location of the road is a constraint on getting across is to miss the

point. Without a road, getting across would be impossible, or at least much harder.[29]

The importance of being conservative

The conservative political philosopher Michael Oakeshott summarised many of these innovation idiocies in the early 1960s (see box). His concern was that 'The Rationalist' (in our context read 'The Innovator' or 'The Management Consultant') put too much store on one type of knowledge (the rational sort that can be written down and analysed) and paid no attention to the second type (tacit knowledge that is embodied in tradition, habit and rules of thumb). People may not even know the reason for doing something in a certain way but, if it has been done that way for years, that may be because it works.

" To the Rationalist, nothing is of value merely because it exists (and certainly not because it has existed for many generations), familiarity has no worth, and nothing is to be left standing for want of scrutiny. And his disposition makes both destruction and creation easier for him to understand and engage in, than acceptance or reform. To patch up, to repair (that is, to do anything which requires a patient knowledge of the material), he regards as waste of time: and he always prefers the invention of a new device to making use of a current and well-tried expedient. He does not recognize change unless it is a self-consciously induced change, and consequently he falls easily into the error of identifying the customary and the traditional with the changeless.

He has no sense of the cumulation of experience, only of the readiness of experience when it has been converted into a formula: the past is significant to him only as an encumbrance . . . He has no aptitude for that close and detailed appreciation of what actually presents itself . . . , but only the power of recognizing the large outline which a general theory imposes upon events.

---

29 R. Nelson, Chapter 2 in John Foster and J. Stanley Metcalfe (eds.), *Frontiers of Evolutionary Economics: Competition, Self-organization and Innovation Policy* (Cheltenham, UK: Edward Elgar, 2001): 24-25.

> With an almost poetic fancy, he strives to live each day as if it were his
> first, and he believes that to form a habit is to fail.**
>
> *Source:* Michael Oakeshott, *Rationalism In Politics* (London: Methuen, 1962).

If you think Oakeshott is being extreme, here's an uncharacteristically
silly aside from the management theorist Clayton Christensen:

> Executives often discount the value of management theory
> because it is associated with *theoretical*, which connotes *impractical*.
> But theory is consummately practical. The law of gravity, for
> example, actually is a theory—and it is useful. It allows us to pre-
> dict that if we step off a cliff, we will fall.[30]

Pity all those poor people who lived before Newton's time, constantly
falling off cliffs because they didn't understand gravity! It's a wonder any of
them survived at all.

Of course, nobody is saying that theory and rationality aren't useful, but
simply that they may be incomplete and should be supplemented by tacit
knowledge and experience. I'd be a bit silly to walk over a cliff after watch-
ing people fall off and listening to my mother tell me not to, simply because
I didn't yet know the theory of gravity.

The common wisdom of innovation is that would-be corporate innovators
should:

- Insulate themselves from all the accumulated history and wisdom
  of their company

- Pretend that they are freelance entrepreneurs

- Work everything out from scratch

All that this achieves is to replace the low-risk, low-return corporate
model with a high-risk, high-return entrepreneurial model. The corporation becomes like a venture capitalist, investing in a range of experiments
most of which will fail. The problem with this approach is that it is simply
not what shareholders want; if they wanted exposure to a venture capitalist, they could invest in one and there's no need for a corporation to do it for
them. Secondly, you come up against the problem of probability. As a corporation you simply can't match the level of experimentation of the whole

30 Clayton Christensen and Michael Raynor, *The Innovator's Solution: Creating and Sustaining
Successful Growth* (Boston, MA: Harvard Business School Press, 2003)

of the external market, so even when you do fund a high number of experiments, you'll probably still find—purely as a result of probability—that someone else will beat you to the killer innovation. And, unless you are very lucky, you will probably find your first few experiments fail completely unless you've linked them to some existing assets of the company that are not available to external entrepreneurs. It's a rare company and unusual corporate executives who then have the stamina to keep going with failures for long enough to get a success, even if they can maintain morale and keep investors and analysts on board while they do so.

Of course the Holy Grail is to combine the benefits of the large corporation with the benefits of being an entrepreneur. This is never going to be entirely possible—large companies can't insulate themselves from the scrutiny and short-term focus of analysts and the media. But, if executives approach innovation understanding the strengths and weaknesses of companies and entrepreneurs, then they can at least go some way to combining the best of both.

Evolution and design

One way of thinking about this is to borrow an analogy from the biologist Richard Dawkins on the difference between evolution and design. Dawkins thought about how a propeller engine could 'evolve' into a jet engine. You'd have to change the engine one step at a time, and each intermediate stage would have to be superior to the ones that had gone before. Dawkins writes:

> A jet engine so assembled would be a weird contraption indeed. It is hard to imagine that an aeroplane designed in that evolutionary way would ever get off the ground.[31]

Clearly, if you want to make a better propeller engine, it makes sense to start with existing designs and do your best to improve them. But, if you want a jet engine, it's best to ignore most of the propeller engine, go back to theory and design from scratch. Most of the designs will probably not work and will certainly be much higher-risk than the propeller engine. But one of them may just be exactly right and much better than any propeller engine could ever be.

31 R. Dawkins, *The Extended Phenotype: The Long Reach of the Gene* (Oxford, UK: Oxford University Press, 1983): 38-39.

Corporations rightly specialise in evolution. They have huge existing knowledge and a network of experts, suppliers and customers to shape and test new ideas. The pressures of financial performance and targets mean that every new proposal must be visibly better than what's gone before. Sensible corporations take advantage of this to do low-risk, highly effective evolutionary innovation.

In contrast, entrepreneurs have none of this evolutionary network to shape and test new ideas. They'd be crazy to go head to head with Unilever by developing a slightly better washing powder. Instead, they must design to achieve something different. This is much higher-risk and most of the time they'll get this wrong, but occasionally they'll get it exactly right. They'll discard the redundant elements of the evolutionary approach, just as a modern-day designer of the human body would get rid of the spleen, which was useful in the past but isn't useful now.

This distinction between evolution and design explains our most important stylised fact—that large companies grow slowly but surely and small companies either fail or grow rapidly. Neither profile is a symptom of failure, but a rational response to the environment that the company finds itself operating in. And investors can invest in a mixture of both to achieve their own desired balance of risk and return.

But, in order to excel and achieve the real Holy Grail of low-risk, high-growth, corporate innovators need to know when they are designing and when they are evolving. What characteristics of a proposed innovation will benefit from the company's history and network, and allow them to make faster, better choices than an entrepreneur ever could? If the answer is none, then they have has no advantage over the millions of entrepreneurs out there. They are imposing unwanted risk on their shareholders and they shouldn't do it.

Similarly, what characteristics will be shaped by the wrong lessons from your corporate history and network? What needs to be insulated from the company and done by design not evolution? If the answer is none, your idea is probably purely conservative and doesn't deserve the name innovation—it is likely to happen anyway through evolution alone. That doesn't mean to say it isn't good, but it won't require much special thought.

Clayton Christensen has done some detailed research on this in his excellent book *The Innovator's Dilemma*.[32] His classic example is of how Canon beat Xerox to the market for desktop photocopiers. Xerox had a fantastic network

---

32 C. Christensen, *The Innovator's Dilemma: When Technologies Cause Great Firms to Fail* (Boston, MA: Harvard Business School Press, 1997).

of sales people who sold huge high-volume copiers to the 'print manager' in big companies. It had an R&D team expert at providing ever greater volume and speed. All of this allowed Xerox to evolve increasingly huge and fast copiers, and its network of relationships provided a valuable defence against any start-up that wanted to compete in the same market.

There was no way that a small desktop copier could evolve in this structure. A desktop copier performed badly on the criteria that mattered to Xerox's existing network of experts, sales people and customers, i.e. volume and speed. Anyone proposing it in Xerox would be asked why they were working on something that was 'worse' than its existing products and which was of no interest to its highest-value customers. The fact that a desktop performed better on other criteria—convenience and accessibility for making a couple of simple copies—simply didn't matter in Xerox's structure and network. It took a small company, Canon, to design from scratch a new machine that would appeal to a wholly new set of customers—small companies and secretaries—who simply weren't visible to Xerox.

We find this story repeated again and again in fields such as mainframe versus personal computers, and hard disks versus floppies. The important point is that Xerox didn't fail because it was lazy, stupid or its staff had insufficiently entrepreneurial ponytails. It failed for pursuing good management practice—listening to its experts and its most important customers.

So, when we're thinking about innovation, we have to know whether our current structures are a help or a hindrance. When we're making decisions about a new product or service, we should consciously be switching gears between evolution and design depending on the specific aspect we're discussing. If we have a new product that is based on our existing technology but would serve new customers through different marketing channels, then our technology meetings should be evolutionary and include all the relevant company technology experts. The marketing meetings should be deliberately intended to design from scratch, and should probably exclude the current marketing department and import some new expertise. And, of course, the converse is true for selling new technology to existing customers.

Our aim is to use both tacit and rational knowledge and to take the best elements from each way of working. If we use only tacit knowledge and tradition through evolution, we'll probably be too conservative. If we use only rational design, we'll be wasting our company's talents and competing head to head with the entire world of risk-seeking entrepreneurs, who unlike us can fail quietly when they get it wrong.

Innovation for poverty reduction

We hope that's cleared the air on the general principles of innovation. But what does this mean for poverty reduction?

We'll start with the most obvious form of innovation that's attracted the most attention and formed the bulk of the 'bottom of the pyramid' bandwagon—designing products and services for poor people.

The problem with evolutionary innovation in rich countries is that it naturally tends to make products more expensive rather than less expensive over time. Engineers love adding complexity and features, and it's natural to create products for the most demanding, richest, least price-sensitive part of the market. It's far easier to listen to real current customers in the developed world rather than potential new customers in the developing world and the criteria that matter to a poor user in a developing country—such as robustness, resistance to heat and dust, low power consumption—may simply not be important to a rich New Yorker. And, once you've created complex products and a high-cost business model, it's difficult to strip costs and complexity out of the system. Simply 'crimping' a product to sell it to poorer people without changing the underlying business model and inherent costs is not a path to sustainable business.

So, when we're thinking about the product itself, it will make sense to adopt a design approach and forget much of what the company already knows from the developed world. Local people—whether as employees, suppliers or partners—will be well placed to design products from scratch that are suitable for local needs and uninfluenced by the unhelpful lessons the company has learned in richer markets. They'll also be cheaper than expensive expatriates, whose wages alone could undermine any attempt to adopt a low-cost business model.

But, as we've identified, if a business is taking nothing but money from the parent company, then it's unlikely to prevail in a market that's full of entrepreneurs all trying different solutions. Innovators have to identify what they want to take from the parent company, and this is perhaps where expensive expatriates—steeped in the knowledge of the business and with a network of contacts—can be useful. Of course, the answer will be different from company to company, but often the strengths of large companies are the abilities to scale up, to create structures and rules, and to operate efficiently without relying on brilliant individuals or corporate heroes. It is these business system skills that can often be added to local innovators to combine locally relevant products with world-class implementation skills.

Widening the scope of innovation

Perhaps the most interesting areas in innovation for poverty reduction are not the product itself but the processes by which customers acquire, use and dispose of it. The elements of a product purchase—discovering its existence, learning how to use it, financing its purchase, getting it, using it, disposing of it—may all be different in developing countries.

The classic example of a company that has prospered by concentrating on these questions is Cemex, the Mexican cement company. One would think that cement wasn't a very promising product for innovation; it's a simple commodity product, produced very close to customers because of high transport costs and with little scope to expand the overall market. But, through a range of innovations during the 1990s, Cemex doubled its profit margin from 10% to 20% while increasing revenue from $2 billion to $6 billion.

Cemex executives spent several months living in the poor districts of Mexico to understand the barriers for people to buy their products. They discovered that many Mexicans went to work in the USA with the specific aim of earning enough money to build a house back home. But the system was imperfect; transferring money from the States was risky and expensive, and you couldn't always rely on your family back home to use the money wisely. So Cemex, which we recall manufactures a commodity product in an industry that traditionally sells to the market around its factory, opened a sales office in the USA. Customers could design a construction project in the USA, select the materials and pay for them in dollars. The cement would then be delivered back home in Mexico.

The Cemex executives also discovered that people often saved for construction projects using a community-level group savings system. Each month, the members put money into the pot and each month one member takes the whole pot. It's not a lottery—you receive the pot according to a strict rota and, over the course of several months, you withdraw exactly as much as you put in. To a rationalist economist, this doesn't make much sense. Why go to so much trouble to achieve the same result as if you simply hid the money under the bed? If you like risk, why not enter a proper lottery? If you don't like risk, why not save in a bank and receive interest? But, as we should learn from Michael Oakeshott, if something has existed in a community for some time, then it's probably useful—even if we don't yet have a theory to explain it. Development economists eventually understood that the community scheme was a useful means of committing to saving; the ritual of putting money into the pot with your friends saved you from wasting the money on drink, cigarettes or other short-term temptations.

Cemex identified that the community-based system was effective in a world of inefficient banking, lack of credit and low commitment to savings, and started to help communities to organise their own schemes. The result was that poor people were better able to save to buy Cemex products and the market increased accordingly. It's an interesting example of Cemex learning that its main competitors for the customer's money were drink and cigarettes rather than other cement products, and then using a real understanding of community dynamics to find a solution that benefited the company and the customer alike. The fact that it increased the savings rate—a key objective in poverty alleviation—was not the aim but a valuable side-effect that improved the company's reputation.

Much of the useful innovation in poverty reduction revolves around identifying what elements are 'missing' from the physical, economic and legal infrastructure of a developing economy and then finding alternatives. Thus micro-credit systems cannot rely on credit ratings and enforceable contracts, so they use the power of community stigma instead. As we discussed in Chapter 4 on inefficiency traps, these solutions may be second-best compared with an effective market economy operating under the rule of law, but they may be better than nothing and may help to kick-start development.

> ""Competitive context has always been important to strategy. The availability of skilled and motivated employees; the efficiency of the local infrastructure, including roads and telecommunications; the size and sophistication of the local market; the extent of governmental regulations—such contextual variables have always influenced companies' ability to compete. But competitive context has become even more critical as the basis of competition has moved from cheap inputs to superior productivity.""
>
> Source: Michael Porter and Mark Kramer, 'The Competitive Advantage of Corporate Philanthropy', Harvard Business Review, December 2002.

Of course, not all innovation need be about the product or the way it is acquired and used. The business model itself and relationships with distributors, suppliers and retailers are also ripe for innovation. In the fast-moving consumer goods company we discussed in Chapter 1, the management realised that they couldn't deliver the low-cost, localised products that poor but numerous potential customers needed. Its fully integrated centralised business run by expensive expatriates simply couldn't meet the demand, particularly as the country did not have an effective distribution network that could reach every village and every small family shop. So it invented a licensing system in which farmers could supply direct to customers and local shops using small-scale company technology under a 'quality assured' brand. The aim was to combine the best elements of the farmer entrepreneur (local knowledge and proximity to market) and the company (technology, quality control and a trusted brand). The company already worked with a network of farmers to increase the quality of its supplies, so the innovation was a natural evolutionary step for the procurement department, but a bizarrely inefficient travesty as far as the manufacturing experts were concerned. The procurement department was allowed to run the project, the manufacturers shut out, and our criteria for the perfect 'conservative innovation' were met.

Provoking innovation

All of these ideas are great with hindsight but how do we provoke some new ones?

There are numerous consultancies out there who claim to make your employees more 'entrepreneurial' and 'creative', and there is no shortage of out-of-work actors who'll run 'workshops'[33] to encourage staff to wear coloured hats and throw balls around. But, as we hope we've made clear, the aim should not be to make your staff more entrepreneurial. This is particularly true if the idea of 'entrepreneurial' is to abandon the accumulated wisdom of the company and proper business analysis, and instead rely on hunches, emotion and commitment. If we accept Michael Oakeshott's argument, then innovation should be treated with *more* scepticism than existing practices. Proposals should be subjected to detailed scrutiny to check that they fit with some element of the company's strengths and aren't simply an entrepreneurial roll of the dice.

What you *can* do with staff is provoke practical ideas by giving them new information. The Cemex practice of asking employees to spend time in the poor districts of Mexico with its potential customers is a valuable and increasingly popular approach to innovation. But it is not the whole story.

---

33 The comedian Alexei Sayle says that anyone involved in a 'workshop' who isn't a carpenter should be shot.

Dare we say that one could have achieved the same results in a more analytical way by discussion with development economists? Buying cement for house construction is a long-term investment requiring a lump sum in the form of savings or credit. A development economist could have identified that formal mechanisms for both are rare among the Mexican poor and described the informal methods that communities have used to fill the vacuum. The economist would probably have done so for free and been open to ideas for joint programmes to solve the problem.

Far from being freed from the 'shackles' of corporate history, corporate innovators need to understand more about their company. What are the ideas that worked and why? What are the strong and weak points of the existing experts, culture and network? Where will my innovation be supported and where will it be killed? What are the hidden gems, such as good procurement practices, that could provide the basis for a new business model? A study tour of the company's existing operations is essential if the corporate innovator is not to become a mere entrepreneur. We do not want to make the mistake that Oakeshott accuses rationalists of:

> To patch up, to repair (that is, to do anything which requires a patient knowledge of the material), he regards as waste of time: and he always prefers the invention of a new device to making use of a current and well-tried expedient.[34]

Flashes of inspiration based on new experiences are great, but so are analysis and strategic thinking. Particularly if one is importing a business model from a developed country, one can systematically identify the essential factors that the existing business relies on and analyse which elements are missing in the new location. What steps must the customer go through to get the product? What do retailers have to do? What infrastructure of suppliers, distributors and partners do we rely on? And, most importantly, in this context, what community, development and business initiatives are there that could deal with the gaps?

Finally, rather than making your employees more entrepreneurial, why not make entrepreneurs more corporate? Why not include local entrepreneurs, partners, suppliers and experts in your deliberations, so that you can draw on their tacit knowledge of the host society? Why not provide *them* with a study tour of the company, so they can understand your priorities and see where the corporate strengths could complement their entrepreneurial skills?

34   Michael Oakeshott, *Rationalism In Politics* (London: Methuen, 1962).

For five major organisations [in Vietnam], manufacturing on behalf of Unilever, the company offered financial support to upgrade equipment and provided extensive training programmes on key issues such as safety and environmental awareness . . .

Working with local businesses has not only helped Unilever achieve significant sales *but it has enabled it to form relationships with local people who understand the market in great detail. This knowledge has been vital in establishing the business* [our emphasis].

Source: *Building Partnerships with Suppliers*, Unilever Insight Sheet, 2004.

Completing the circle:
from the poor back to the rich

Consider the story of the microwave oven and videocassette recorder industries. Companies fought ferociously to offer sophisticated product features. Most products ended up almost identical—and over-designed from the customer's perspective.

Most buyers found the features confusing and irritating. They even expressed fear about using the products because of all the controls and flashing lights. Companies outdistanced one another but were off-target in giving buyers what they wanted—simplified microwave ovens and VCRs at low prices—and achieving a low-cost structure.

It is the drive to achieve a leap in value with a low-cost business model that makes companies question everything an industry and competitors are doing. It opens their eyes to the difference between what industries are competing on and what the mass of buyers really value and how they can provide that at a low cost.

Source: W. Chan Kim and Renée Mauborgne, *Think for Yourself: Stop Copying a Rival*, Financial Times Summer School, 11 August 2003.

Innovation experts such as the INSEAD professors Chan Kim and Renée Mauborgne have compellingly identified the dangers of providing increasingly complex and expensive products to consumers. Clayton Christensen identified the dynamics behind the process—a natural tendency to rely on technical experts and existing major customers who always want faster, bigger, better even when that leaves the rest of us behind. In response to this cycle, there are numerous examples of successful start-up businesses challenging the incumbents by concentrating on poor, under-served or new customers by stripping out rather than adding in features.

The trap of producing ever more expensive and complex products is made additionally dangerous because the simpler products that are initially launched to serve the unattractive bottom of the market or the invisible new customers eventually improve so much that they can eventually capture all of the market—again think of desktop computers versus mainframes.

Anyone who's been to IKEA on a Saturday afternoon would not say that it was a better experience than a full-service high street furniture shop. It's out-of-town, inconvenient, hard work and they don't even build the damn things for you but expect you to do it yourself. How can the founder possibly be one of the richest men in the world? The answer is that he identified some expensive elements of the existing furniture trade—convenience and service—that could be stripped out so that the savings could be divided between better design, price cuts and profits. This new combination of benefits and costs was attractive to a sophisticated but not rich group of customers who were willing to spend their Saturdays making sense of bizarre self-assembly diagrams in return for low-cost good design.

And while we're on the subject of the world's richest people, in 2004 *Forbes* magazine placed Karl Albrecht, founder of Germany's Aldi discount supermarket chain, as fourth richest. Aldi is doing the same for food that IKEA did for furniture.

All of this research on the power of 'disruptive innovation' has been done in the developed world with no thought for anything but maintaining the operations of rich-country incumbents. The management experts have rightly identified the problem that evolutionary innovation in rich countries tends to lead to greater complexity and expense, creating a gap for start-ups at the bottom of the market. But, as we've identified, the solution of ignoring existing industry practice and designing from scratch makes one no better than an entrepreneur. The IKEA founder was brave to build his first store based on his insight that customers would value a different package of costs and benefits, but what if he'd been wrong? It would have been an expensive mistake.

It won't surprise you to learn that innovating in poor countries is one elegant solution to the innovator's dilemma. If the rich-country environment leads your evolution astray and you think that design is too risky, why not change the environment that you evolve in? A different environment will lead you to different solutions. The natural pressures of innovating for a poor market will tend to force the company to find simple, low-cost, robust solutions that over time can reach sufficient scale and quality to be introduced back into the bottom of the rich market.

> "The most successful emerging market companies start with low costs, but differentiate themselves on speed to market and innovation. The Chinese appliance manufacturer Haier, for example, enjoys a reputation for rapidly launching high-quality new products tailored to the needs of local consumers. Innovations include washing machines that clean vegetables as well as clothing for sale in some rural provinces. Haier has extended its new product development to western markets, featuring wine coolers, mini refrigerators and freezers in the US and Europe."
>
> Source: Donald Sull, *Financial Times*, 5 August 2005.

The management scientist Peter Williamson describes a company that achieves this sort of thing as a 'meta-national'. The multinational model is simply to export the headquarters' model to poor countries because you want their markets or cheap manufacturing capability. The communication is all one-way—from HQ to poor-country outpost. In contrast, the meta-national learns from all its operations in different environments and the role of headquarters is to organise the transfer of knowledge between all the outposts. In our terms, this is an attractive model of conservative innovation. The way to find new solutions is to evolve in several different environments simultaneously and then spread the successful innovations around.

Follow-up questions

What strengths do you bring to your market? What do you bring to your market that are strengths at home but may be weaknesses or irrelevancies in the developing world? How do you make sure you use the strengths of your company without being constrained by the weaknesses or the irrelevancies?

What do customers value in your market? Do you know? What do they need do to acquire, finance, use and dispose of your product? Can you help them with any of those elements? What are NGOs and the government doing to fill the gaps? Could you help or benefit?

What are entrepreneurs doing in your market? How could you co-operate?

How do you resist your head office's efforts to make your products increasingly complicated? Can you use the discipline of a developing market to simplify your products and your business model? What should head office be learning from you?

Further reading

The Innovator's Dilemma: When Technologies Cause Great Firms to Fail by Clayton Christensen, published by Harvard Business School Press in Boston in 1997, is a classic account of how companies miss opportunities at the bottom of a market. *The Innovator's Solution: Creating and Sustaining Successful Growth* by Christensen and Michael Raynor (published by Harvard Business School Press in 2003) rehashes some of the material but also proposes some rigorous ways to analyse new opportunities and overcome the dilemma.

'Value Innovation: The Strategic Value of High Growth' by Renée Mauborgne and Chan Kim in *Harvard Business Review* (January/February 1997) talks brilliantly about reinventing the combination of value and cost for consumers. As of March 2006, it was available as a paid download at http://harvardbusinessonline.hbsp.harvard.edu. Their book, *Blue Ocean Strategy*, published by Harvard Business School Press in 2005, expands the idea.

From Global to Metanational: How Companies Win in the Knowledge Economy by Yves Doz, Jose Santos and Peter Williamson, published by Harvard Business School Press in 2001, discusses how companies can replace a 'top-down' model of international management with a network of outposts which all learn from each other.

Open Innovation: The New Imperative for Creating and Profiting from Technology by Henry Chesbrough, published by Harvard Business School Press in 2003, discusses the difficulty for companies of matching the level of experimentation in the market and recommends ways of capturing external innovation.

For links to these resources and other relevant material, go to www.makepovertybusiness.com.

8

Making the changes

A lot of this book is simply about the need for expatriate managers to be cleverer about the way they engage with their host country. And perhaps the most immediately profitable business case we'll make is to argue that companies should be better at selecting, training and managing their expatriate managers. Improved performance in this field would lead to immediate savings in the costs of premature repatriation, underperformance in the job and high staff turnover. It would also lead to a new breed of expatriate managers being appointed who are sensitive to the needs of their host country and so better able to implement the type of recommendations we make on reducing poverty.

The statistics on expatriate performance are frightening. A significant percentage of expatriates cut their postings short. Many of those who stay underperform. And those few who are any good and last the course then become unsatisfied back home and leave to join a competitor. It's a bleak picture, but at least it offers hope for improvement. When we find examples of companies failing to contribute much to economic development or poverty alleviation, it may not be anything inherent in the nature of capitalism or globalisation, but simply that the people currently charged with implementing company strategy in developing countries are not up to the job.

❝A fully-loaded expatriate package including benefits and cost-of-living adjustments probably costs anywhere from $300,000 to $1 million annually, probably the single largest expenditure most companies make on any one individual except for the CEO. The fact is, however, that most companies get anaemic returns on their expat investments . . . We found that between 10% and 20% of all managers returned early because of job dissatisfaction or difficulties in adjusting to a foreign country. Of those who stayed for the duration, nearly one-third did not perform up to the expectations of their superiors. And perhaps most problematic, one-fourth of those who completed an assignment left their company, often to join a competitor, within one year after repatriation.❞

Source: J. Stewart Black and Hal Gregersen, 'The Right Way to Manage Expats', *Harvard Business Review*, March–April 1999.

❝An alarmingly high expatriate failure rate exists at all corporate levels.
    The obvious direct costs of failure such as overseas compensation, allowances and repatriation are high, but they are not the most serious. The real costs are the indirect costs such as damaged relationships with the host-country government, with local organizations and with direct customers, not to mention the potential loss of product market share.❞

Source: Marvina Shilling, *HR Magazine*, July 1993.

Companies make a series of mistakes when managing expatriates. The first and most obvious is the decision to send an expatriate at all. Why? What do we want them to contribute that could not be done by a local? Clearly, if we get this question wrong, or don't consider it at all, any rational decisions on selection or training will be impossible.

Having identified why we're sending someone, a decision on selection should be much easier. But all too often companies send someone abroad as a reward, forgetting that performance in the home environment won't necessarily predict good performance elsewhere. There's a tendency to choose people based on their technical proficiency rather than on their ability to operate in different cultures.

Much of the training that budding expatriates then receive is either ineffective or counterproductive. Perhaps many readers have been on a 'cross-cultural' course in which you're told not to put the soles of your feet on the table with your left hand while burping, or whatever. While there are some nuggets to be found in this sort of thing, it's always struck us as rather quaintly old-fashioned and patronising, and ignores the fact that the person across the table you're dealing with may indeed be a 'foreigner' but may also happen to have several masters' degrees from Harvard and be well used to the ways of rude foreigners.

> ""Having a global attitude is not the same as being able to imitate local styles. It's just as important for managers to be themselves. I spent 17 years working for a Swiss company as a US resident. In the 1970s it was considered forward in Switzerland to address people by their first names. But with my peers and subordinates I followed the US standard of using first names. People were okay with this because they knew I was not being false.""
>
> *Source:* Fred Hassan, Chairman and CEO, Schering-Plough, quoted in: S. Green, F. Hassan, J. Immelt, M, Marks and D. Meiland, 'In Search of Global Leaders', *Harvard Business Review*, August 2003.

At the other end of the training spectrum, expatriates might be sent on security courses run by ex-army officers who stride around in Timberland desert boots giving over-firm handshakes. We went on one once, admittedly before going to Iraq, and we were treated to videos of kidnap victims having their fingers chopped off. The main lesson we drew was never to stray from our cosy English villages ever again and, if we did go abroad, then never have anything to do with the locals. It certainly didn't give us any idea that we could enjoy a posting and strike up positive relationships with local people.

The strategic decision: why send an expatriate?

In Chapter 7 on innovation we discussed the importance of understanding what the corporation would contribute to the local market and what the local market would contribute to the corporation. In this context we need to ask: 'what is the role of the expatriate in combining the best of the company with the best of the local market?'

- Is the expatriate there to apply the efficient management systems of the corporation to a chaotic but potentially productive local business?

- Is the expatriate there to learn from the local market and apply the lessons more widely throughout the company?

- What elements of corporate practice are fundamental to the success of the company and non-negotiable, and what elements can be adapted for the local market?

- What does the company 'know' that it wants to transfer to new markets?

- What would the company most like to learn from its presence in new markets?

These are serious strategic discussions and, unless you have them, it's impossible to identify whether or not to send an expatriate at all. Of course, the answers also begin to give some guidance about who to send. And, for the executive about to be sent on a posting, they're good questions to ask as they will define your freedom of manoeuvre and give you some clues on what would constitute a successful posting.

> To succeed, multinationals must modify their business models for each nation. They may have to adapt to the void in a country's product markets, its input markets, or both. But companies must retain their core business propositions even as they adapt their business models. If they make shifts that are too radical, these firms will lose their advantages of global scale and global branding.
>
> *Source:* Tarun Khanna, Krishna Palepu and Jayant Sinha, 'Strategies that Fit Emerging Markets', *Harvard Business Review*, June 2005.

A further possible reason for sending expatriates abroad is simply to improve them as international managers. The Group Chief Executive of HSBC, Stephen Green, puts it as follows:

> No one gets to the top of HSBC without having worked in more than one market. If you look at the executives currently running the company's largest businesses, all of them have worked in more than one, and nearly all in more than two, major country markets. We strongly believe, as many others do, that travel broadens the mind. And if travel alone does that, just think how

much more you get from living and working in different countries.[35]

If this is the main objective, then clearly the posting has to be part of a coherent career plan and attention paid to repatriation and retention. And of course the personnel development objective cannot be divorced from the fundamental strategic question of what exactly the company hopes to learn from different markets and how it will apply those lessons across different markets. There is no point in developing internationally aware managers if you do not have an understanding of what you want them to do with their international experience or if you cannot motivate them to stay with you by putting their international skills to productive use.

"One international company decided to reduce its costs by cutting the number of expensive expatriates it employed around the world by one quarter. The decision was taken at main Board level but had to be implemented by the international HRM manager. 'No business manager was prepared to tell me that he was running an unsuccessful operation,' he said, 'so the only thing we could do was to "localise" some of the jobs.' Within two years he had achieved the objective: at around the same time, the company realised that while some of the local replacements had been obviously successful, some of the changes had been—equally obviously—disastrous. Over the next few years the company began to increase the number of expatriates again. 'Of course,' the IHRM manager said, 'we shouldn't have started with a decision on numbers; we should have found some way of working out which jobs needed to be filled by expatriates and which didn't. We've tended to do it mainly by intuition.'"

Source: Dr Hilary Harris (Director of the Centre for Research into the Management of Expatriation), 'The Changing World of the Expatriate Manager', *Management Focus* 13 (Winter 1999); www.som.cranfield.ac.uk/som/news/manfocus/content13.asp, 20 March 2006.

We once took part in a seminar with a mining company that was considering what it most needed to know in order to succeed in its business over the next 25 years. It recognised that its technology was unexceptional but believed that it was good at 'politics'. When we probed further, we realised that what this really meant was that it was good at getting permission from

---

35 Quoted in: S. Green, F. Hassan, J. Immelt, M, Marks and D. Meiland, 'In Search of Global Leaders', *Harvard Business Review*, August 2003.

sheikhs and presidents-for-life to dig holes. It was certainly not good at dealing with democracies, municipalities, tribal groups, the media, public opinion and all the other emerging elements of an increasingly complex international system. Yet the company selected its innovation projects based on what it needed to learn about technology and located them in the places that would be easiest for it politically, thus ensuring that it would not learn the things that it most needed to know. The conclusions of the seminar recommended the opposite—that the company should deliberately seek out politically difficult places in order to start learning about the complexities of the modern world. By the end of the seminar, the participants realised that they'd made some crucial progress—only now could they begin to make proper decisions about which expatriates to post where.

Selecting an expatriate

"Companies that manage expats wisely do not assume that people who have succeeded at home will repeat that success abroad. They assign international posts to individuals who not only have the necessary technical skills but also have indicated that they would be likely to live comfortably in different cultures."

Source: J. Stewart Black and Hal Gregersen, 'The Right Way to Manage Expats', *Harvard Business Review*, March–April 1999.

"Research into criteria of effective international managers consistently highlights the importance of 'soft' skills such as self-awareness, flexibility, intercultural empathy, interpersonal skills and emotional stability. However, surveys of international selection practice within organisations show that most rely on technical competence as a prime determinant of eligibility."

Source: Dr Hilary Harris (Director of the Centre for Research into the Management of Expatriation), 'The Changing World of the Expatriate Manager', *Management Focus* 13 (Winter 1999); www.som.cranfield.ac.uk/som/news/manfocus/content13.asp, 20 March 2006.

The strategic decision on what you're sending an expatriate to do will of course determine some of the specific competencies you're looking for in a candidate. These might not only be technical capabilities in marketing or engineering, but also the extent to which they have contacts and credibility within the parts of the home company that you want to connect to the new market.

But there are also some generic skills that are useful for all expatriates. The experience of being posted from head office to a distant outpost is principally one of loss of formal control. When you sit in the headquarters of a large corporation, you deal mostly with colleagues from within your own organisation, with whom your relative responsibilities and authority are reasonably clear. You tell subordinates what to do and you do what your boss tells you. You have power over your suppliers and your customers have power over you. The primary change with moving abroad is that you deal with a far greater number of people where the lines of authority are thoroughly ambiguous or non-existent, and you can't just tell people what to do. What power relationship do you have with a minor supplier who is also the President's cousin? When a journalist desperately wants an interview with you on your CSR programme, which one of you is in charge? Many of the annoying people whom you are isolated from in head office—the government, the media, civil society, the public—suddenly loom large in your everyday work as an expatriate manager.

In this context, we are looking for expatriates who understand informal influencing skills as well as formal authority and rules. The British Diplomatic Service understands this sort of thing well; diplomats have very little formal authority to do anything at all in their host country, so must rely on skills of building trusting relationships and exercising informal influence. When a friend of ours was interviewing graduate candidates for the Diplomatic Service, he'd always ask for some anecdote about when they had persuaded someone to do something for them. One excellent candidate gave a great example—he consistently took an interest in his college porter's[36] stamp collection and, in return, was allowed to sneak into college late at night when the gates were officially closed. The triviality of the story is not important; what matters is that the candidate gave evidence that he had the sort of character that naturally enjoyed understanding and influencing people who were different from him.

The second quality we are looking for is a mature attitude towards rules and procedures. An expatriate, far away from home, has to know what rules to stick to and what rules to break. Operating in their own little fiefdom with little day-do-day oversight from head office, expatriates have to stick

36 This being the British Diplomatic Service, there were inevitably a lot of Oxbridge applicants.

diligently to procedures that are important for the company's reputation and legal standing. But they should not blindly pursue standard operating procedures written for an entirely different country environment if breaking them would result in a much better overall outcome. Making these fine judgements is a tall order.

You have to find someone who is, in some ways, more willing to stick to the rules than average and not exploit the freedom of being away from head office to make merry with the company's long-term profits and reputation in the interests of this year's bonus. But, in other ways, you want the expatriate to be more rebellious than average and not be a slave to irrelevant head office guidelines. In the strategy jargon, the perfect expatriate has to be a living embodiment of the balance between global integration and local responsiveness. Again, the British Diplomatic Service is quite good at managing this balance, as diplomats adhere to rigorous codes of personal conduct but are also keen to make local decisions whenever necessary; any decent ambassador will grandly say 'I am an envoy, not a messenger boy' when given excessively strict instructions from London. In selecting expatriates with these qualities, it is again useful to ask for anecdotes from their professional or personal lives about when and why they have broken the rules.

If this all sounds a bit difficult to quantify or put into a human resources (HR) competency framework, then that's because it is. The Diplomatic Service does use a small amount of psychometric testing and other more quantitative techniques as contributing evidence for a selection decision, but the final decision is made after a series of interviews with experienced diplomats and other professionals who have a real feel for what it's like to operate abroad. When conducting Diplomatic Service interviews, good interviewers would always have in the back of their minds some basic questions but then would just get people to tell stories about their lives. They'd want to know:

- 'Does this person use informal networks to get what he wants, as well as functioning effectively in established hierarchies?'
- 'Has this person influenced people who are different from him?'
- 'What are this person's values? Where does he draw the line?'
- 'Is this person curious? If he was in a restaurant, would he want to know what the people at the next table were eating?'

** Anybody that has read the literature on the characteristics of an expatriate or other international manager cannot fail to be amused at the voluminous pages of competencies and personality characteristics required to ensure successful performance. To take an example, Harris and Moran (1996) tabulate 68 dimensions of overseas success of which 21 dimensions are deemed the most desirable. As Heller (1980) puts it: a flexible personality, with broad intellectual horizons, attitudinal values of cultural empathy, general friendliness, patience and prudence, impeccable educational and professional (or technical) credentials—all topped off with immaculate health, creative resourcefulness, and respect for peers. If the family is equally well endowed, all the better. **

Source: Joe Jordan and Sue Cartwright (Manchester School of Management, University of Manchester), 'Selecting Expatriate Managers: Key Traits and Competencies', *Leadership and Organization Development Journal* 19.2 (1998): 89-96.

** Consider the approach taken by the vice chairman of Huntsman Corporation . . . Over the last five years, Jon Huntsman Jr has developed an informal but highly effective method for assessing cultural aptitudes in his employees. He regularly asks managers that he thinks have global management potential to accompany him on international business trips, even if immediate business needs don't justify the expense. During such trips, he takes the managers to local restaurants, shopping areas and side streets and observes their behaviour. Do they approach the strange and unusual sights, sounds, smells and tastes with curiosity or do they look for the nearest Pizza Hut? Do they try to communicate with local shopkeepers or do they hustle back to the Hilton? **

Source: J. Stewart Black and Hal. B. Gregersen, 'The Right Way to Manage Expats', *Harvard Business Review*, March–April 1999.

Training an expatriate

Given the alarming statistics on expatriate failure, there's a surprising dearth of relevant training courses for international executives. There's certainly a burgeoning business for security firms who train executives on how not to be kidnapped, but these courses tend to see security as an end in itself rather than as a means to doing business. As we discuss in Chapters 5 and 9 on security and reputation respectively, the implementation of short-term or paranoid security measures can often increase the risks they are designed to decrease because, by cutting the company and its executives off from the local community, they lead to resentful neighbours and isolated, stressed, ineffective executives.

While some companies help their executives to deal with immediate security risks, they rarely do anything to prepare executives and their families for the wider stresses of being abroad, despite the huge expense to the company of a manager cutting short a posting or just remaining and doing a bad job. And companies that are obsessive about meeting their duty of care to home-based employees are surprisingly bad at meeting the unique welfare needs of their expatriate staff and families—perhaps because expats are seen as being on a 'cushy number'.

The problems of managing stress abroad are similar to the problems of managing security. You have to find a way of resolving the short-term symptoms without exacerbating the long-term causes or undermining business effectiveness. The classic way for expatriates to manage stress is through extremely heavy drinking, and it's an approach we've often personally championed. But, of course, it's hardly a sustainable route to a happy life and a successful business career. Similar escapist methods such as surrounding yourself with fellow expats, constantly scouring old copies of *The Times* and making repeated journeys home may also make you feel better in the short term, but they only increase the sense of isolation in the long term and do nothing to help you implement the measures we discuss in this book.

❝ If the definition of expatriate failure is expanded to include not only incidents of premature return but also poor work performance, sociocultural adaptation and psychological health, it is safe to say that a majority of expatriates, at least temporarily, exhibit major adjustment difficulties . . . When confronted with strong culture and language barriers, expatriates resorted to coping strategies that reduced stress but also proved detrimental to job effectiveness and long-term adjustment in the host country. ❞

Source: Professor Günter Stahl, *New In Town: How Expats Effectively Cope* (INSEAD Working Paper 2001/77/ABA; Paris: INSEAD, 2001).

Training can contribute to teasing out and dealing with many of these issues, but only if it is underpinned by a clear understanding of what real benefits the company, the manager and the family can get from the posting. A frightening list of all the bad things that can happen abroad and a simplistic account of the potential avoidance mechanisms, unconnected to the realities of the core business and the pressure to perform, will probably be worse than useless. Training courses certainly need to tackle the basics of personal and company security, but in a proportionate way that understands the 'hearts and minds' questions we discuss in this book. The problems of stress management and general well-being need to be discussed not only for managers but also for their families who will be much more involved in the success or failure of a posting than they would be at home (and companies of course have to deal with a modern world in which partners have careers that they might not want to give up and it is no longer considered natural to send the kids off to boarding school). Finally, expatriates will need training in specialist disciplines such as crisis management, media relations, public affairs and all the other issues that are the job of someone else at home but fall to the generalist expatriate manager abroad.

Managing an expatriate

The social performance manager of an oil company once told me that his biggest problem was managing the different time horizons of expatriate managers and host communities:

> When one of our managers promises that the company will *never* do something, what they mean is that it probably won't happen over the course of their posting. In ten years' time when the company does that thing, the manager has got his bonus and is well away, but the community remembers.

Much of what we recommend in this book is about getting expatriate managers to do extra work and to take extra risk in the short term in order to secure higher long-term profits at lower long-term risk. In addition to the problem that the benefits may accrue after the country manager is no longer around to gain the credit, many of these benefits may also be extremely difficult to measure. Our friendly oil company community manager put the problem of measurability as follows:

I asked our managers how they knew when they'd succeeded with the local community. Our guy in the Middle East said he knew he'd won when he sat up all night in the desert with the locals, eating roast goat and gossiping. Our man from Latin America said it was when he ran a successful football tournament—company versus town on the first day and mixed teams the next. Now, if you're so clever, you tell me how to find a single global measure that captures all that.

Creating incentives for executives to contribute to the general long-term health of the company while also achieving measurable short-term goals is of course one of the fundamental problems of management, and we're not going to solve it here. But what we can do is consider how the gap between head office and a foreign outpost can exacerbate the problems and suggest some ways to deal with them.

There are two basic elements that make management difficult. The first problem is whether you can totally define the outcome you want and then observe whether it has been achieved. Clearly, if you want to manage people to pick apples, you can just observe the number of apples they produce and pay them accordingly. But, in most companies, you're looking for a more complex mixture of outcomes, some of which will be more measurable than others. The second problem is that most companies want to pay people for the effort and intelligence they put into a problem rather than just the outcome and, in particular, you do not want to punish them for failures that were outside their control. Again, if you're paying people for picking apples there's a fairly direct correlation between effort and outcome, so there's little problem. But, in the real world of management, you may not want to punish someone who's done the right thing all year but then the country is struck by an earthquake—and the challenge then is whether you're able to observe that they are indeed doing the right thing.

In the apple-picking case, management is trivial—you pay per apple and effectively you have a market relationship with your employees. But the companies that adopt this approach (e.g. investment banks who pay bonuses based only on financial results each year) find it very hard to interest their executives in also contributing to innovation, teamwork, reputation or other long-term issues for the bank. There is also little sense of an implicit contract in which the bank will protect you in a bad year that was out of your control. What this means is that bankers get sacked in bad years and demand all the money they made for the company in good years.

Most companies do not want to work on this basis. They aim to incentivise their employees to contribute to a range of outcomes and they aim to smooth their employees' income by assuming some of the risk of operations. This is why management becomes difficult—and the problems come down to the extent that you can accurately observe the outcome and then whether you can assess how closely that outcome was linked to effort rather than random or uncontrollable factors. When everyone's operating in the same head office, it's relatively easy to apply these sort of judgements and, in particular, to modify the hard facts of annual financial performance and targets with some more nuanced judgements.

- 'He didn't reach his targets but that was because of the recession'
- 'She did reach her targets but only by taking huge risks with the brand'
- 'They're not team players'

One can also constantly modify expectations and targets throughout the year based on a shared understanding of the changing market and the company's values and direction.

This sort of nuanced management is much more difficult to do when expatriates are managing in a market that is unfamiliar to the bosses in head office and their everyday activities are invisible to them. In this sort of environment, vague exhortations from head office to 'improve our reputation', 'engage with the locals', 'increase local procurement', 'contribute to the UN Global Compact' or 'get some political support' are unlikely to have much weight compared with short-term financial targets. Why should a shrewd expatriate manager waste much time on these issues when lack of local procurement can be blamed on 'hopeless locals' and poor political relations on 'country risk'? Head office have very little way of distinguishing between expatriates who are genuinely trying to do the right thing in a complex environment and those who are hiding behind the complexity to ramp up short-term profits and their own bonus at the expense of long-term profitability and risk management. Head office has little evidence available to it other than the financial figures. When a country manager says, 'there simply are no competent local suppliers', how on earth do you know whether he's looked properly?

It might be tempting simply to add in more targets such as achieving a certain percentage of local procurement, but we are not convinced that this is the answer. As we've outlined in other chapters, what matters is not only the fact of local procurement but the quality of it.

- Is the supply contract with a 'usual suspect' who is as easy to find and as expensive as an international supplier and who will do little to widen one's political support?

- Is the procurement an arm's-length arrangement or one that transfers some skills?

- Is the purpose of local procurement only to reduce costs or also to enhance reputation?

There comes a point where you simply can't write enough meaningful targets to capture all these different issues.

The ultimate solution to this is to do as HSBC do and develop a cadre of senior managers who all understand a range of difficult markets. They're then much better equipped to judge what is realistic to expect from a country manager and to see through excuses. Companies whose most senior people have never been abroad and who send managers off for a short stint overseas without using their expertise on their return will find it impossible to deal with the nuances we are discussing here, and will be in thrall to the country manager who'll always say, 'It's all very difficult over there. You don't know what it's like.'

Of course, developing an international cadre of managers takes time. In the meantime, management reviews can be informed by a 'balance sheet' approach to assessing performance in a foreign outpost. What has the manager 'borrowed' from the reputation and knowledge of the group and from the legacy of previous country managers? And what has this manger 'invested' in terms of building up reputation and knowledge which can continue to be used in the country and also transferred to the rest of the group? The specific elements of this assessment should be based on the strategic understanding of the *purpose* of having an expatriate in the post, but the sort of questions that might be asked include:

- Has the manager implemented programmes that have been copied elsewhere in the group or praised by external experts and publicised by the group?

- What has changed about the reputation of the country operation?

- What does the manager know now that he didn't know at the beginning of his posting and how has he communicated that around the group?

If we were being really professional about this, we'd commission an audit at the beginning of a manager's posting and again at the end. It would examine what contribution the company was making to the local economy and how well that was understood and communicated. It would examine the reputation of the company with a cross-section of local people from the farmers next door up to the President. It would examine not only the volume of local supply but the diversity of local suppliers. And, crucially, it would benchmark the answers not against global 'best practice' or the group's performance elsewhere in the world, but against other multinational companies operating in country. Of course, the purpose of such an audit is not simply to judge a manager's performance. It also sets an agenda for the manager and identifies any particular reputational or country risks that need to be managed.

As we outline in Chapter 9, it makes sense to commission a local think-tank or similar organisation to conduct such an audit and to examine a cross-section of multinational companies rather than ask only about one's own organisation. A general survey of multinationals' reputation and contribution to development by an independent outsider is more likely to generate honest results than a company person wandering round saying 'how are we doing?'

Repatriation

""One fourth of those who completed an assignment left their company, often to join a competitor, within one year after repatriation. That's a turnover rate double that of managers who did not go abroad. We know of one company that over a two-year period lost all the managers it sent on international assignments within a year of their return—25 people in all. It might just as well have written a check for $50 million and tossed it to the winds.

Good companies end expatriate assignments with a deliberate repatriation exercise. Most executives who oversee expat employees view their return home as a non-issue. The truth is, repatriation is a time of major upheaval, professionally and personally, for two-thirds of expats. Companies that recognize this fact help their returning people by providing them with career guidance and enabling them to put their international experience to work. ""

Source: J. Stewart Black and Hal Gregersen, 'The Right Way to Manage Expats', *Harvard Business Review*, March–April 1999.

"" For many expatriates, the impact of 're-entry' can be more traumatic than the initial culture shock at the start of the assignment.

Organisations need to pay careful attention to the way in which they handle repatriation for two key reasons. Firstly, the cost of losing someone who is dissatisfied with his or her position on return is significant, both in purely financial terms and also in terms of the investment in human capital. Secondly, and perhaps more importantly, expatriate assignments are crucial tools in the effort to create a transnational mindset in the organisation. Failure to disseminate the individual learning gained from a foreign assignment to others in the organisation is a clear barrier to the goal of becoming a truly global operation. ""

Source: Dr Hilary Harris (Director of the Centre for Research into the Management of Expatriation), 'The Changing World of the Expatriate Manager', *Management Focus* 13 (Winter 1999); www.som.cranfield.ac.uk/som/news/manfocus/content13.asp, 20 March 2006.

"" How Ya Gonna Keep 'Em Down on the Farm (After They've Seen Paree)? ""

Source: Chorus of a song written by Sam M. Lewis and Joe Young (music by Walter Donaldson), published in 1919 by Waterson, Berlin & Snyder Co., Music Publishing.

Perhaps the worst day of my (Peter's) life was a week after I returned home from a long-term posting in Indonesia. It was raining, it was midnight, I was standing at a bus stop near Leicester Square in London waiting for a night bus home. Where was my driver? Why was I going home at all, when my friends back in Indonesia would be at parties that went on way past midnight? What had happened to the 'me' that was a big fish in small pond now that I was a 'nobody' in London? It didn't help that I'd spent the working week getting lost in a building that had been redesigned since I was last there; failing to get into or understand new computer systems; and being told what to do by people who seemed important but whom I didn't know. Nobody seemed very interested in what I'd learned while in Indonesia and nobody was very clear about what I'd be doing now. But they did all tell me I was 'very lucky' to have done what I'd done.

Is it possible to sue an organisation for showing you paradise then taking it away from you?

A repatriation exercise needs to do three basic things. It has to help expatriates and their families adapt to the practical and personal stresses of return. It has to help expatriates fit back into the company and find a useful role. And it has to capture what expatriates have learned while they've been away. A training course can contribute to solving the first two problems and, in particular, can help expatriates to learn about the several years' worth of changes that have happened while they've been away. But the third element, capturing what the expatriate has learned, has to be much more than a self-contained exercise. Returning expatriates have to be able to continue contributing to the company's strategic effort to learn from developing markets and to combine the best of head office with the best of country outposts. This might mean contributing to strategy sessions, it might mean mentoring other expatriates, or it might mean recording their experiences and feeding it into innovation teams or change managers.

What's this got to do with poverty alleviation?

The section of our audience interested in development might have lost interest by now. What has all this internal management stuff got to do with poverty alleviation?

We find that many development people, especially the ones who are most opposed to business, tend to think that companies are super-competent entities that precisely enact a well-defined strategy. When companies fail to do something good, or do something very bad, it must be because the company is evil or because the profit motive drives it down the wrong path. We can see this in all the development writing about establishing backward linkages to local companies—the business case seems so obvious that development people are baffled that it doesn't happen more often.

Of course, anyone who has worked in business knows that most employees of multinationals are well-meaning people struggling to get things done in imperfect institutions. Innovation mostly happens despite the system rather than because of it, and the existence of a good business case is absolutely no guarantee that something will be implemented.

The types of action we want companies to take on poverty alleviation are precisely the sort of innovations that are difficult for companies to implement. The benefits are often long-term and intangible, whereas the costs and risks are immediate and clear. The people expected to implement the changes are not necessarily equipped to deal with the ambiguities of doing business in a foreign culture and might just be scared to emerge from their corporate ghetto. Their incentives and targets may all be short-term and they may adhere to them more rigidly than their head office counterparts because they're not benefiting from nuanced guidance from their bosses.

So, when development people see companies taking little action to improve their contribution to development, they should not assume that the business case has been carefully considered and rejected. They should aim to understand the constraints and incentives that the expatriate is working under and construct the development case accordingly. They should help the expatriate understand the local environment and they should look for opportunities to 'de-risk' initiatives such as local procurement by helping expatriates to meet the right locals. Ultimately, expatriates might just need a little reassurance and hand-holding rather than a wholesale reinvention of the capitalist paradigm.

Follow-up questions

Why are you sending an expatriate? What do you want them to do?

What are your figures for performance and retention of expatriate staff? Are they worse than for your home staff? Why?

Are your expatriate staff clever enough and open enough to implement the ideas in this book? Do you need to be better at selection and training?

What's non-negotiable in your business model? What is open to local variation? Have you told your expatriate managers?

What do you know that you want to apply to a developing country? What do you want to learn? Is your expatriate manager the right person to do that? Will your expatriate managers be able to apply the lessons when they return to head office?

Has your expatriate policy changed since the days when partners didn't have careers and kids automatically got carted off to boarding school?

Have you agreed with your expatriate managers what progress is required on reputation, localisation and learning? Are you able to measure progress? Do you have a way of balancing the pressures of short-term financial targets?

Further reading

'The Right Way to Manage Expats' by J. Stewart Black and Hal. B. Gregersen, in *Harvard Business Review*, March–April 1999, gives an excellent account of the expatriate management cycle. As of March 2006, it was available for paid download at http://harvard-businessonline.hbsp.harvard.edu.

'Strategies That Fit Emerging Markets' by Tarun Khanna, Krishna Palepu and Jayant Sinha in the June 2005 issue of *Harvard Business Review* discusses the need to adapt business models to local markets or to support the development of local infrastructure to fill the gaps. As of March 2006, it was available for paid download at http://harvardbusinessonline.hbsp.harvard.edu.

For links to these resources and other relevant material, go to www.makepovertybusiness.com.

9

Reputation and country risk

" For hapless foreign investors, the web of Suharto's patronage held the key to success in Indonesia. The list of those who succeeded is a who's who of international business including BP, PowerGen, British Gas, Mitsui, Itochu, General Electric, Edison International and Siemens. Now, just ten days into the post-Suharto era, those links have become a curse. "

Source: Financial Times, June 1998.

" It takes twenty years to build up a reputation and five minutes to ruin it. "

Source: Warren Buffett.

The *Financial Times* report about the fall of President Suharto in Indonesia captures the paradoxes inherent in most major companies' approach to country risk in developing countries. The more you try to minimise your risk by getting close to the current regime, the more the new regime will want to undermine you. The more you compensate yourself for your risk by negotiating higher returns or fixing the returns in hard currency, the more you'll be seen as a blood-sucking profiteer when the political climate changes. The more you surround yourself with bodyguards and fences, the more the local community will hate you. Your attempts to decrease your short-term risk end up increasing it in the long term, and all of these paradoxes combine to create the greatest risk of all—that you will be described as 'hapless' in the *Financial Times*.

After Suharto's fall, many international companies had their contracts torn up or renegotiated under much less favourable terms and, in some cases, their parent group's share prices suffered as a result. Some companies rescued the situation with a mixture of hasty political pressure, CSR and philanthropy, but only after several weeks of panic and negative publicity.

Clearly, no company wants this to happen, but there is a widespread assumption that problems like these arise only at times of extreme and rare political change and that, in most countries for most of the time, you can protect yourself from country risk as long as you've got decent lawyers and fixers and have covered your currency risk.

But that's simply not the case. In Indonesia, the transition was briefly frightening but not particularly extreme, and the new President was a pro-tégé of Suharto. The international utilities companies that were the main target for cancellation of contracts had well-drafted 'take or pay' contracts with payments guaranteed in dollars. But that didn't stop the new regime from cancelling the payments. The harsh reality is that, regardless of the law, if a country can't pay then it won't pay—particularly if the contracts are seen as the unjust leftovers from a previous corrupt regime and if the prices to the consumer are politically sensitive. At a time of a plummeting local currency, it's simply impossible to outsource your financial risk to the local people, no matter how close you were to the previous President.

And it wasn't just Indonesia. In the late 1990s, multinational companies faced confiscation of assets and cancellation of contracts in Pakistan when Nawaz Sharif replaced Benazir Bhutto, and in India when the anti-liberali-sation BJP party replaced the Congress party in several state governments. These changes were a result of regular elections rather than a rare moment of turmoil and, in India, the BJP were simply implementing what they'd already promised to the electorate. The contracts that came under threat were less manifestly unfair than some of those that were challenged in Indonesia and less obviously based on patronage. So doing the right thing is not necessarily a protection if you get caught up in a power struggle between the outgoing and incoming regime, as in Pakistan, or become the target for populist attack, as in India.

The Collaboratory [sic] for Research on Global Projects at Stanford University studied 33 power projects in emerging markets during the 1990s and found that only 12 of the 33 contracts in the sample actually held. Of the remainder, two were cancelled, eight were unilaterally renegotiated, and 11 were renegotiated with mutual consent from both government and private parties. Ryan Orr from Stanford says that

> over the long lifecycle of an infrastructure project negotiating power slowly shifts from the private investor to the host government. Initially, the government offers attractive terms because they need private investment, technology or management expertise. But once the infrastructure is operational and the host has attained what it desires, the foreigner suddenly appears not to be so essential. The government takes advantage of this new bargaining leverage and enacts changes in terms and conditions that range from gradual erosion of revenue streams to forceful expropriation of the asset or property site. And because infrastructure assets are not easily redeployed, the investor is trapped.

While such government opportunism is clearly important, he adds that their may also be other factors:

> the debt-like nature of many of the investments lead to payments problems in times of economic crisis, many agreements are with sub-national entities which are less concerned with the overall impact of conflict over contracts than are central governments, allegations of corruption and undue pressure by home governments make the fairness of agreements suspicious, problems of regulation in natural monopolies are difficult to solve, and, perhaps, spreading democracy accelerates conflicts between hosts and investors.[37]

The common response to these risks is to become more of a political expert and to pay for political expertise by subscribing to country briefings or employing some ex-ambassador to turn up to meetings now and again. But, as people who've traded as political experts ourselves, we're sceptical of this approach. The first problem is that real experts, if they were honest, would

---

37   R. Orr, 'Investment in Foreign Infrastructure: The Legacy and Lessons of Legal-Contractual Failure', February 2006; http://crgp.stanford.edu/membership/presentations/gcr2/Orr_Final.pdf, 24 May 2006.

acknowledge the extreme difficulty of predicting political change in any country. We well remember sitting in a seminar at the Royal Institute of International Affairs in early 1991 while *the* world expert on the Balkans explained why there would never be a war there. And before the fall of President Suharto, all the experts in Indonesia agreed that the main criteria for a successor were that he would have to be an ex-army officer and would have to be from the island of Java. Fine—except that Suharto's actual successor turned out to be a civilian from the island of Sulawesi. As the economist John Kenneth Galbraith famously said: 'There are two classes of forecasters: those who don't know, and those who don't know they don't know.'

The more fundamental point about business people trying to behave like political experts is that, even if your information and analysis is correct, what do you actually do with it? What levers are available to you when you learn that the Minister for Administrative Affairs was out of favour last week, but is back in favour now? Is there any specific action you can take? Probably not. Wouldn't you rather just be getting on with your core business rather than playing politics?

Your political expert will probably advise you to employ a powerful local partner to protect you from harm. Back in the Suharto days, we had a conversation with a senior manager from an international utility company in Indonesia along these lines:

'Are you worried about political risk?'

'No no. We've got the President's son on board.'

'What's the payback period on your project?'

'Twenty years.'

'Did the President's son mention that his Dad will be in his mid-nineties by then? Longer than any Javanese man has ever lived? So, even if he dies peacefully in office, he won't be around when you need him.'

'Oh. Bugger.'

Not exactly the most sophisticated political analysis, but it was enough to confound this businessman's political strategy to protect a multi-million-dollar project. Sure enough, not only did the son lose all his influence when his father fell, but he also ended up in prison for murder. One of the abiding mysteries of political risk is that companies that are extremely sophisticated about their political relations in stable law-based democracies become blundering idiots when operating in far more dangerous and unstable environments abroad. These days, very few regimes stay in place for the length of the payback period of a major project and, in a world that is slowly but steadily democratising, the few presidents-for-life still knocking around cannot be relied on to last much longer.

Why on earth do business people continue to think they can accurately pick a local to fix everything for them, despite the evidence that the practice is often useless and sometimes counterproductive? Do they really think they can predict how the political scene will develop over their project's payback period and, more importantly, that they can specifically predict how their chosen favourite will fare over that time? Do they really want to be closely associated with someone over whom they have no control and who by definition is likely to be a controversial figure?

> For all their might, for all the vast economic resources they command, these organisations [MNCs] so crucial to the spread of western-style capitalism have invariably struggled to understand, predict, and shape the social and political environment in which they operate in developing countries—even though the nature of this environment may underpin, or undermine, their commercial success in the long run. Time and time again, in a pattern which is too pronounced to be coincidental, the western multinationals have exercised their power in unplanned, unsophisticated or self-defeating ways . . .
>
> Companies have tended to focus their attention, and their best brains, on narrow economic issues—such as how best to market their goods or to boost profits from year to year—rather than the social and political environment in which they do business, even though neglecting this, or failing to understand it, has often damaged their interests in the long run. Many multinationals today still think of this non-economic context as merely a 'public relations' issue; or instead they categorise any problems as 'political risk', suggesting they are simply beyond their control.
>
> Source: Daniel Litvin, *Empires of Profit: Commerce, Conquest and Corporate Responsibility* (London: Texere, 2003).

Perhaps there is an analogy with stock market day traders who believe that they can weigh all the evidence and pick specific stocks which they predict will outperform the market. There's loads of evidence that it's impossible to consistently make better-than-average returns by this method, but perhaps it's nice to believe that you can predict the future even if it involves you in lots of redundant work. In contrast, sophisticated investors don't convince themselves that they can predict how individual stocks will behave. Instead, they put together a risk-balanced portfolio of stocks that will protect them however the future turns out. Then they relax and sneer at all those would-be experts who spend their time and money on tip sheets, gossip and analysis.

We advocate a similar approach to country risk. How do you develop a portfolio of people who will be able to protect you regardless of how the political future turns out so that you can forget about politics and get on with your real business? Instead of staking everything on your ability to pick the 'right' local fixer, how can you spread your risk across a range of local supporters, from the farmers next to your factory up to the emerging political elite? How can you 'outsource' your politics to local people rather than wasting time trying to become an expert yourself?

You will not be surprised to learn that the methods we recommend in this book are a good way to develop a wide range of support for your activities. If you are tightly embedded in the local economy and seen to create value for a wide range of people, then you will be supported in times of trouble and a new regime will think twice before unravelling your operations. If your employees fell well treated and well trained, they're likely to tell their friends. If the local farmer supplies his crops to your canteen, he's unlikely to burn your factory down. If the local steel magnate makes much of his profits from selling to you, he's unlikely to tell his local politician to block your operations. You're not relying on any one of these people to do all the work, you're hedging your bets across all of them.

This approach is very different from corporate philanthropy. If all you do is give money to unconnected charities, any new regime knows that it can always dismantle you and invite in some new company who can also be persuaded to dole out cash to the local orphanage. The aim instead is to use the core business to create a unique source of value to the local economy which cannot be easily copied or replaced—we call this a **Development Value Proposition**. Just as you would seek to differentiate your Customer Value Proposition and protect the difference with some sustainable competitive advantage, you should try to do the same with the value you're seen to create for the local economy. In Chapter 3 on poverty measures, we discussed how to present your economic contributions to expert audiences in development agencies and governments. In this chapter we focus more on public relations and public affairs exercises that will work with non-experts among the public, local business and politicians.

Establishing your Development Value Proposition

- **Customer needs.** What are the priorities for economic development valued by your host government, development agencies and non-governmental agencies? Clue: your local World Bank office should be able to provide information on this and many countries now produce a Poverty Reduction Strategic Plan.

- **Understanding how your product meets those needs.** How does your presence in the country contribute to these economic development priorities? Can you put figures on the most important elements? Do your target audiences understand and appreciate your contribution?

- **Defending your advantage.** What unique assets, competencies and networks allow you to deliver these benefits? How can they be defended and developed?

- **Developing the value proposition.** Can you use these competencies to deliver further benefits?

- **Communicating the value proposition.** Do your employees, advisers and contacts understand the value proposition? Is it clearly communicated in your marketing and public affairs activities? How can you dramatise and illustrate it?

Where do you start with all this? What parts of your operations should you start publicising as creating significant value for the local economy? The following quote from the economist Professor David Henderson[38] gives us some clues:

> How might one try to estimate the contribution that a business makes to the general welfare over any given period? An obvious answer is: by putting a value on the benefits that arise from its operations, and then subtracting from this the estimated associated costs. Now the benefits to people in general are indicated—not precisely measured, but clearly indicated—by what they are prepared to pay for what it produces and sells—that is by the revenues accruing to the business. On the other side of the balance, the costs to people in general are the value to them of what could have been produced if the resources that the business used had been deployed elsewhere; and a good first approximation to this unknown figure is the actual costs of the business. Profits are the

---

38   D. Henderson, *Misguided Virtue: False Notions of Corporate Social Responsibility* (Hobart Paper No. 142; London: Institute for Economic Affairs, 2001).

difference between the two flows, revenues minus costs. Hence they are a prima facie measure of the good that a business is doing for people in general. That is why they have an essential signalling function in a market economy. That they typically accrue to shareholders is not the point. The argument for treating profits as an indispensable first-approximation measure of an enterprise's contribution to the general welfare has the same force, and the same rationale, when the businesses concerned are publicly owned.

For a business enterprise, whether private or public, to concern itself directly and predominantly with profits is not to show undue regard for owners as distinct from 'stakeholders' in general, to slight other worthy objectives, or to allow greed to govern its actions. It means focusing on the most obvious measure of the value to society of what that enterprise is doing. The idea that a firm's true or main contribution to 'society' has to arise from other aspects of its motives and conduct, not directly related to the profitability of what it does, derives from a basic misunderstanding.

In a perfect world, you'd simply attach this quote to your income statement and your public relations work would be done. But in the 250 years since Adam Smith made a similar basic argument, the public have been remarkably resistant to it, perhaps because it seems so counter-intuitive. So each company has to make it again for themselves, and dramatise it to make it credible and real.

"Companies have to demonstrate that our presence, particularly in the poorer countries, is a source of human progress."

Source: John Browne, Group Chief Executive, BP, speaking at Harvard Business School, 3 April 2002, quoted in G.C. Lodge, 'The Corporate Key: Using Big Business to Fight Global Poverty', *Foreign Affairs* 81.4 (2002).

"When we first went to China we just built some factories and tried to sell things. We got nowhere. We started again, went to the Government and asked how we could contribute to the country's development. That's what successful Chinese business people do. Since then we've thrived.

Western managers should realise that in many countries there is a much closer connection between Government and business than they are used to.

> You have to convince the Government that what you are doing fits their plan for the country.**
>
> Source: expatriate manager, multinational FMCG company.

It may seem odd to look to your areas of greatest profit to publicise as your greatest contributions to society. The most profitable areas are where you're charging the highest prices and pinning down your suppliers to the lowest costs. Wouldn't it be better to brush these tricky subjects under the CSR carpet? Perhaps you should publicise your least self-interested actions, presenting yourself as a fabulous charity that routinely undercharges and overpays before apologising for any residual profits by giving them away.

We believe that this CSR approach is fundamentally inconsistent and unsustainable. It means you have to make arguments to investors (about your ruthless profitability) that are different from the ones you make to everyone else. Anyone who advocates this approach in a company will ultimately be sidelined by a management who are legally obliged to focus on shareholder interests and profits. And, most importantly in this context, governments and informed publics recognise that it's unsustainable and simply don't believe in it any more.

> **As a consumer and a citizen I must say that neither hamburger chains sponsoring youth football teams nor the occasional recycled envelope impresses me much. Companies should drop this fashionable farce. Or at least call it by its proper name: marketing.**
>
> Source: Ingvild Paulsen, letter to The Economist, 5 February 2005.

What would it be like to cut through this web of CSR evasions and half-truths and start celebrating your profits as David Henderson recommends? When considering your Development Value Proposition to the local economy and how you should publicise it, what would happen if you started by looking at the biggest items on your income statement to identify the priority areas?

The first things that you might spot are those sources of high profits which you really should be embarrassed and worried about. These are the economic old chestnuts of externalities and monopoly power which, as David Henderson later acknowledges in his paper, sometimes make profits an inaccurate measure of social value. If you can charge high prices because you've bribed the government to give you a monopoly or because the economy is under-developed and you don't yet have any competitors, then your revenues are reflecting your artificial market power more than the fundamental value you're creating for customers. Similarly, if you make money because you pour all your waste products into a river, thereby imposing the costs on your neighbours rather than incurring them on your own income statement, then your profits have become meaningless as a measure of social value.

You should be worried about these partly because you're a nice person, but mostly because these sources of profits are likely to be unsustainable and are likely to attract criticism. Perhaps the subtlest and most common form of country risk is simply that the economy liberalises and develops around you, destroying your artificial market power and the sources of these high profits. As in the example in Chapter 1, the risk is that because you're a foreigner you won't notice these developments until it's too late and head office are complaining about your declining profits.

Holders of artificial market power face attack from all sides. Economies are liberalising under pressure from consumers, donors, the World Bank, the IMF and the World Trade Organisation (WTO). Local competitors are getting cleverer and gaining access to international capital and expertise. And, if you're in the consumer goods market, you can be sure that major retailers will seek to break your market power so that they can negotiate away your margin.

Over time, your cosy monopoly is likely to be swept away by a mixture of regulatory and competitive pressure. And, even if you do manage to hold on to your control thanks to a temporarily powerful local fixer, will it survive a change in the political climate or attack from an even more powerful local who wants a piece of the action? As an outsider, should you be basing your main source of profits on your ability to understand and control local politics against the wishes of consumers, trade customers, foreign governments and international organisations? Is that really a sustainable competitive advantage?

We recall here that, when the incoming Indonesian government tore up various multinationals' contracts, the relevant embassies and international bodies felt obliged to complain at the breach of law. But many of our friends were the ones who did the complaining, and they did so ever so gently with the clear implication that the breaches were understandable and were unlikely to face much international criticism. Most of our friends believed the contracts had not been beneficial to the Indonesian people and so were not inclined to make too much of a fuss, regardless of the formal instructions from their headquarters.

So artificial monopolies, whether through local government support or a short-term absence of competitors, are unlikely to be sustainable. Your job as a country manager might be to milk them in the short term, but you owe it to your shareholders to replace them with something more sustainable in the long term.

How about the externalities you impose on the environment and on society? Are they any more sustainable than your monopolies? Probably not. Developing countries are receiving huge sums of money from donors to improve their ability to regulate business and are coming under scrutiny if they corruptly fail to do so. And, of course, the Western consumer is increasingly interested in a company's behaviour elsewhere in the world and willing to punish wrongdoers at the expense of the company as a whole.

> The real power of the American consumer has not yet been unleashed. The heads of Burger King, KFC and McDonald's should feel daunted. They're outnumbered. There are three of them and almost three million of you. A good boycott, a refusal to buy, can speak much louder than words.
>
> Source: Eric Schlosser, *Fast Food Nation: The Dark Side of the All American Meal* (Boston: Houghton Mifflin, 2001).

The point here is not the familiar one that your environmental or social destruction is an externality that you impose on society but which is not measured in your company's accounts. You may or may not care about that. More importantly, your negative behaviour as a country manager imposes a risk on your overall parent company that is not measured in your local accounts. You are creating a negative externality for your shareholders in order to seize the short-term gain of operating in an under-regulated or corrupt economy. As in the case of monopolies, as a country manager you owe it to your shareholders to find more sustainable, accurately measured sources of local profits.

So we've identified that relying on monopolies or externalities is bad long-term business as well as bad for development. By examining your accounts with this in mind, you can spot the areas of operation that may not be sustainable and which create your greatest sources of reputational and country risk. As a country manager, you should be seeking to replace these short-term tactics with some long-term strategic advantages and, if you describe it to your head office in these terms, they should support you.

Once you've stripped out your artificial advantages, what's left in your accounts is the market economist's dream—profits that accurately represent your benefit to society. These are the areas you should be expanding and publicising.

How does this work in practice? Well, take a look at your accounts and identify the most profitable areas, which are also perhaps the reason you set up in the country in the first place. If you're able to pay low wages to people and still have them turn up to work, that must be because the alternatives on offer to them are even worse. Are you taking people out of unemployment or unskilled jobs, training them and giving them the tools to produce valuable items? Are you helping to develop efficient low-cost suppliers, who also supply other industries in the country? If so, you had better start publicising it before someone looks at half the story and just criticises the low wages and low prices you pay. Similarly, if you're achieving high prices for your products, it must be because they're highly valued. Do consumers welcome what you do, or do local industrial companies use your products or services to create further value? What are you contributing to the local economic ecosystem by supplying quality goods and services? Are you helping to create a local infrastructure which attracts further foreign investors? And how about the balance of payments for those items you export? Again, you should start publicising these questions before your enemies tell half the story of your 'excess' profits.

It is odd that companies miss the opportunity to make a case on the basis of their economic impact. In its audit of HSBC's 2004 CSR report, the consultancy Corporate Citizenship said:

> We believe that future reports should also show more clearly HSBC's economic impacts. Companies' primary role is to create wealth through the provision of goods and services: reliable and efficient global financial systems, in particular, bring many benefits to personal and business customers. In our view, greater analysis of HSBC's direct economic impacts and the wider effect they have would improve understanding of the company's contribution to society, alongside its continued response to the full range of stakeholder concerns.

This is right. HSBC's CSR report outlines the company's various philanthropic, environmental, social and employment initiatives. Separately, its Annual Report boasts of its profits to shareholders and financial analysts. The two perspectives are rarely brought together, and nowhere is there a proper analysis of how operating an efficient banking system benefits an economy. This is an odd omission for a company that has long operated effectively in a far wider range of developing countries than most of its competitors. HSBC are above average, but not exceptional, in an analysis of CSR in the banking sector for the Dow Jones Sustainability Index,[39] perhaps because it is easier for their competitors to achieve good corporate governance and environmental efficiency as they operate mostly in the developed world. Why don't HSBC pick on the area where it does have a competitive advantage and focus far more on its positive economic impact in developing countries?

It can be a good idea to commission a local think-tank to conduct this sort of economic impact research. Not only do you develop understanding directly with some bright young things, who often go on to be eminent in government, you also present a much more credible case to the wider public. And you should resist the temptation to be centre-stage when you deliver the results. The media will find the press release 'Widgets PLC is excellent' eminently resistible. A locally run seminar on economic development, poverty and the role of international investment may be much more attractive and credible and, as a funder, you can be included as one of the case studies. You may also find a range of local and international partners, including donor agencies, to help shoulder the costs and put together a good guest list.

> " In 2004 we conducted research in a joint project with Oxfam to explore the links between wealth creation by companies such as Unilever and poverty reduction in Indonesia. "
>
> Source: Unilever Social Report 2004
> (www.unilever.com/Images/Social_Report_LoRes_NoBleed_tcm13-13259.pdf, 20 March 2006).

Finally, you need to make sure all of your employees know the story and can communicate it. They'll probably be more motivated if they feel they're contributing something to the local community but, just as importantly, they're the face of your company to outsiders. When you're in London or New York, it's easy enough to lock people away at corporate headquarters so that all dealings with the press are filtered by the public affairs department. But, in your operating countries, you just can't keep your deputies from getting drunk with a local politician or journalist at some dreadful embassy party, and you'd better make sure they have the company's Development Value Proposition off by rote.

39   SAM Research Inc., October 2004.

For a good example of how to communicate all this simply and effectively, have a look at Unilever's Social Report 2004 available from the company's website (www.unilever.com). The report includes a graphical representation of the value Unilever creates for suppliers, employees, consumers, shareholders and governments, and unashamedly links its profits to social progress.

Creating value: not just at the beginning

We have argued for the importance of global business houses keeping one eye on the objective of the reduction of poverty when starting or expanding an investment in a developing country. But what happens when an investment ends? What happens when a time-bound project comes to a close or an operating business is wound up? The answers to these questions have strong implications for the effects on poverty of business operations—and strong implications for the reputation and the bottom line of MNCs.

Let's start with an obvious example—a time-finite resource extraction project. What should a global mining house do once the 20-year life of its tin mine is up? Most likely, the mine has produced considerable local income throughout the life-cycle of its operation. Jobs have been created, directly and indirectly, taxes paid, locally and nationally, and suppliers have benefited from guaranteed contracts paid in hard currency. And then, one day, the mine stops operations. The jobs are lost, tax payments cease, supply contracts terminate. The economic shock is large and sudden. It is not at all impossible for much of the wealth generated by the mine over the preceding 20 years to be undone if no plan for the certain eventuality for mine closure is in place. And, not only that, if the owner of the mine has current or potential operations elsewhere in the country or elsewhere in the world, then reputation and economic risks are a real problem. The entire profit from the mine over its lifetime, or more, could be lost if a problem at one mine makes it impossible to secure licences elsewhere.

In such a case, miners (the same might apply to a large timber logging project) need to plan carefully for the poverty effects that the end of their project will have. There are several strategies that can be pursued. One involves the use of trust funds. The idea is to save funds for inter-generational benefits. There are a few challenges with this. First, the funds, since they are collectivised, need to be well managed, not squandered and not subject to corrupt leakages. Secondly, the approach presupposes that investment opportunities in the future are better than those of the present. Thirdly, it also presupposes that the needs of the future generation are equal to or greater than the present. These conditions will often, but not always, apply.

Another approach is to place strong emphasis on the development of 'secondary', 'downstream', 'alternative' or 'backwardly linked' businesses. The idea is, through deliberate policy and business decisions, to create a network of connected businesses that, over time, develop a life and business cycle of their own and gradually reduce their dependence on the original core business. A further option for business is to consider closing the business down slowly, giving the local market more time to react. It is important to note, however, that, almost invariably, businesses in developing countries dependent on a 'nodal' investment are 'sticky' when reacting to signals that a business will be winding down. A company may send a false signal to the market by suggesting that it will wind down its business sooner or faster than it really intends to with the aim of trying to catalyse action by affected populations and businesses.

Other techniques available to MNCs in a situation where their business is closing include:

- Training and retraining for local businesses so they can direct the use of their capital toward the production of other goods or services

- Selling small parts of their business to local enterprises with medium-term contracts to ease the adverse wealth effects of the economic restructuring

- Investing in new viable local businesses in alternative industries

- Assisting in relocating staff to new locations and with finding new jobs

There are different examples to draw from over recent history. When closing down or downsizing a business, Tata in India, for example, often simply keep staff on its payroll, but not on its business premises. This is good for reputation, good for wealth distribution in a poor country, and helps avoid industrial relations problems. Placer Dome's gold mine in the highlands of Papua New Guinea has a multi-year plan to ease the local economy around the gold mine into other business areas during the mine's winding-down period. The proposed effect of the plan probably won't work fully, but it will make the blow to local poverty rates less than if the company didn't do anything at all. Smart companies will start planning an exit strategy right from the outset. This is good because it will increase the chances of success and because they will be able to say afterwards that they did at least plan for the problems.

This issue is also important for large-scale contracting firms buying from concentrated locations, particularly for brand-name garment and textile buyers. If Nike suddenly stops buying garments from a particular factory in Vietnam, the localised business costs and, subsequently, the poverty effects can be profound. Such business decisions may sometimes be necessary or inevitable, but the poverty effects in poor countries can be large and need at least to be taken into consideration in business decision-making.

Case study: Wal-Mart and economic development

To try to bring out some of these lessons on reputation and economic contribution, we'll take a look at Wal-Mart's operations and reputation in the USA. The lessons we learn from a country that supposedly welcomes private enterprise and understands free markets will be doubly applicable in developing countries that are still deciding whether business is a good thing.

These are treacherous waters. Wal-Mart is widely loved and widely hated, and we've no wish to bring demonstrations, lawsuits or odium upon ourselves. But we chose Wal-Mart precisely because we can learn from the dramatic and legitimate differences of opinion they face. We hold them up as a company who do some things well and some things badly, rather than as a boring and uninstructive example of best practice.

First the good things: 82% of American households buy something at Wal-Mart or Sam's Club in a typical year. In 2003, Wal-Mart came top of *Fortune* magazine's poll of most admired companies and, in 2004, there was consternation when it slipped to 'only' 4th place. In 2004/05, its philanthropic foundation gave $170 million (or $5 every second) to charity, making it the biggest corporate donor in the USA. And, not least, Wal-Mart made $10.3 billion in profits in 2004/05 which, if we take David Henderson's view, is a lot of value created for the community.

“Wal-Mart is the greatest thing that ever happened to low income Americans. They can stretch their dollars and afford things they otherwise couldn't.”

Source: W. Michael Cox, Chief Economist, Federal Reserve Bank of Dallas, 'Is Wal-Mart Good for America?', *The New York Times*, 7 December 2003.

“[Wal-Mart's] efficiency is the envy of the world's storekeepers.”

Source: Andrew Edgecliffe-Johnson, 'A Friendly Store from Arkansas', *Financial Times*, 19 June 1999.

And yet Wal-Mart is widely hated too. It faces class action lawsuits for gender discrimination and abuse of hourly pay. Store openings in California have been delayed or stopped by a series of legal actions. A Google search of the phrase 'Wal-Mart sucks' produces 283,000 results, and you can read any number of employee and supplier horror stories at the inevitable www.walmartsucks.org website.

What explains these widely differing views? Our guide in these treacherous waters will be the independent economist, Dr Emek Basker of the University of Missouri, who has published two peer-reviewed academic papers on the impact of Wal-Mart on local and national economies in the USA. Our aim is not to come to some definitive view on Wal-Mart's overall 'suckiness', but to explore some of the economic arguments that Wal-Mart make and to learn lessons from Wal-Mart's own assessment about how well it has presented its case.

Wal-Mart's basic argument is that it creates jobs and offers low prices. Its advocacy website (www.walmartfacts.com) puts it as follows:

A UBS Warburg study found that Wal-Mart grocery prices are 17–20% lower than other supermarkets, which has the greatest benefit for a community's low-income families. According to a study done by the Los Angeles Economic Development Council, Wal-Mart potentially saves individual families more than $500 a year. This is money that can be used to buy food, gas or any other priorities for that family.

Studies show that new businesses spring up near Wal-Marts and existing stores flourish as they take advantage of the increased customer flow to and from our stores. Drive by any Wal-Mart store and count the number of businesses operating nearby, many are independent local businesses or locally owned franchises. The most definitive look at this issue, by Dr Emek Basker at the University of Missouri, showed average increases of 50 retail jobs in communities five years after the entry of Wal-Mart.

In fact, this is only part of the story. Basker's original paper[40] says:

> I find that Wal-Mart entry increases retail employment by 100 jobs in the year of entry. Half of this gain disappears over the next five years as other retail establishments exit and contract, leaving a long-run statistically significant net gain of 50 jobs. Wholesale employment declines by approximately 20 jobs due to Wal-Mart's vertical integration.

So, on average, Wal-Mart creates jobs in its own store but destroys them in nearby retail stores and *local* suppliers, creating a net benefit of 30 *local* jobs per store. The number of jobs created or lost in suppliers elsewhere in the USA and abroad is not measured.

On the question of low prices, the results are less ambiguous and clearly in Wal-Mart's favour. Basker says:

> I find robust price effects for several products, including shampoo, toothpaste, and laundry detergent; magnitudes vary by product and specification, but generally range from 1.5–3% in the short run and four times as much in the long run . . . These results have real implications: if the market basket of low-income shoppers declined by this full amount, the income effects could be very large.

Basker attributes this change to simple competition: Wal-Mart is able to charge lower prices because it is more efficient and, as a result, local competitors either match the prices or go out of business.

There is, however, another possible argument which Basker describes as follows:

> The aggregate mechanism works through Wal-Mart's interactions with both suppliers (manufacturers and importers) and other large retail chains. This mechanism can lower prices in communities not served by Wal-Mart if it leads to lower costs for other retailers. The argument for this mechanism is as follows. By

---

40   Emek Basker, University of Missouri, 'Job Creation or Destruction? Labor Market Effects of Wal-Mart Expansion', *The Review of Economics and Statistics* 87.1 (February 2005): 174-83.

demanding lower prices from suppliers, Wal-Mart forces manufacturers to cut costs, possibly by relocating overseas. Competing
retail chains (notably Target, but also many smaller chains) also
increase efficiency by emulating Wal-Mart's innovations in logis-
tics and distribution. The result is lower prices in chain stores
across the country, some in locations that have no Wal-Mart
stores.

This argument is harder to make and, in fact, Basker finds no evidence for
decreasing prices in areas that do not have a Wal-Mart. But this does not kill
the underlying argument. Other retailers may be benefiting from better
efficiency but, in the absence of Wal-Mart's competition, are choosing to
keep the gains rather than pass them on to consumers.

Unsurprisingly, the advent of Wal-Mart has created winners and losers.
Value that was being captured by small-time retailers, a unionised workforce and US suppliers is now captured by (often poor) consumers and
cheaper overseas suppliers.

°°There's no question that workers without skills find it difficult to get
paid as well as they once did, that employers are more reluctant to supply
comprehensive health benefits, and that Chinese imports are pummelling
American manufacturers. Wal-Mart thrives in part by contributing to or
piggybacking on each of these trends, but they were all well underway
before Wal-Mart took the United States by storm. Who should we blame
for the other 90 percent of Chinese imports?

Wal-Mart is a mere pass-through for its customers—one that takes a
slim margin for the trouble. At Wal-Mart, the customer is king, everyone
else be damned: competitors, employees, and the domestic manufacturing
base. Everything Wal-Mart does—particularly its low prices—is done in the
name of slavish devotion to consumer demand. And every day, millions of
Americans ratify Wal-Mart's strategy by shopping there. Stores don't kill
economies, consumers do.°°

Source: Daniel Gross, 'Don't Blame Wal-Mart for the Wal-Mart Economy', Slate, 8 October 2003;
available at www.slate.com/id/2089532.

In general, economists are not neutral about how the economic pie is
divided and would tend to side with Wal-Mart. Economists normally welcome a transfer of value from companies and employees to consumers, and
they often advocate regulatory action such as anti-monopoly legislation to

ensure it happens. The reason for this is that individual consumers have less power than companies or trade unions and so, in general, the balance has to be redressed by legislation and regulation. Similarly, most economists reject protectionist arguments and see great benefits from international trade. And, if we are interested in poverty alleviation, surely we should welcome the export-driven growth of China and other countries.

Perhaps what makes this case difficult is that the vehicle for the transfer of power from companies to consumers is itself a powerful company. And, of course, there are all sorts of non-economic problems with the power of Wal-Mart: for example, many people prefer the community feel and aesthetic qualities of small shops even if they aren't willing to pay the higher prices necessary to maintain them. Finally, all the economic theory in the world doesn't help if newspapers and websites are full of tales of errant Wal-Mart managers abusing their employees.

What are we to learn from all this? Some quotes from Wal-Mart officials give us clues:

> What we found is that there is a different group of stakeholders today that are important and that is a person who's not familiar with Wal-Mart stores, they're not familiar with what we stand for. So their view of Wal-Mart stores is what they read in the newspaper and what they see on TV. We have decided it is important for us to reach out to that group.[41]

> For too long, we thought that if we just focused on our customers then everything else would follow. We probably did not realize soon enough how important it was to work with the media. It is an acknowledgement that the media and others offer important venues for telling our story, and we need to continue doing a better job at that.[42]

> If you think of us being one of the largest food retailers in the United States—most of the food that we have in our stores, over 90 percent I am told, is made or grown in the United States. It's about $40 billion. If you think about the fact that we're building 50 million square feet of stores just in Supercenters—it doesn't include distribution centers; it doesn't include the variety of neighborhood markets that we have and just what we call Division One

41 H. Lee Scott, Wal-Mart Chief Executive, *New York Times*, 9 September 2004.
42 Mona Williams, Wal-Mart spokesperson, *New York Times*, 9 September 2004.

stores, the stores that don't have food—it's over 50 million square feet a year [total]. The jobs that are created just in construction alone are 40,000, 45,000 jobs a year, and about $5.5 billion of product bought that goes into [those] stores, whether it's carpet on the floor or ceiling tiles or lights or toilets in the bathroom or plumbing fixtures — that is significant. We likewise estimate that in information technology, we support roughly 20,000 jobs in America. We do no outsourcing of our information technology at Wal-Mart. And the list goes on . . .

What I can't tell you is that I created X numbers of jobs that way or what the dollar amount is. We understand the importance of being able to convey that. We're trying to get a handle on it [our emphasis]. But I can tell you the numbers are significant, and all you have to do is walk in a Wal-Mart store and see all of that is sold. We are the biggest purveyor of pet food and the biggest purveyor of shampoos, and that stuff is made in America.

We are creating a lot of American jobs, and that is on top of the fact that we have 1.2 million workers of our own. So this is an economic engine that's all about creating jobs in America. It's not just about buying things [from] China.[43]

The message is that pleasing consumers and doing good global economics may convince economists, but economists don't get elected. To convince everyone else you need to analyse, dramatise and communicate the benefits to your *local* economy, and you need to do so before rather than after the complaints start coming in. Consumers are surprisingly unhelpful in all of this, because a large number of slightly happy but unconnected consumers are no match for a small number of very unhappy and well-organised trade unionists and former suppliers. This is a long-standing fact of political life about the difficulties of galvanising large groups of dispersed people, which explains why lobbyists can often push through measures like monopolies and tariffs that benefit the few at the expense of the many.

The obvious economic arguments you can make are around jobs and competitive pressure on prices, but this is mostly about a different division of the existing economic pie (or a zero-sum game if you prefer the jargon). As we've identified, this creates both winners and losers—and the losers may be more organised and more influential than the winners (try putting your

---

43   Ray Bracy, Wal-Mart's vice president for federal and international corporate affairs, 'Is Wal-Mart Good for America?', PBS, 16 November 2004.

current Chinese supplier up against your former American supplier on American TV and see how far you get). It's an important but difficult battle to win, and you'll need good evidence and good advocacy skills.

The subtler argument is that you are also expanding the size of the pie. This is about the skills and efficiency that you have introduced into the sector as a whole to the benefit of consumers, suppliers and even competitors. It is an even harder argument to make and requires some serious analysis. Ultimately, however, it might be the most convincing to policy-makers and opinion-formers and the one that puts you least at odds with other powerful groups. It is also the core development argument for the benefits of your activities—you are providing growth not redistribution.

" Wal-Mart's policy is to pay hourly associates for every minute they work. However, with a company this large, there will inevitably be instances of managers doing the wrong thing.

Wal-Mart disputes the allegations in this [gender discrimination] lawsuit and believes that certification of the case as a class action is improper because the claims of six plaintiffs are not representative of the experience of women working at Wal-Mart. Wal-Mart is seeking reversal of the class certification decision. Wal-Mart does not tolerate discrimination of any kind. Wal-Mart is a great place for women to work, and isolated complaints that arise from its 3000+ stores do not change this fact. "

Source: www.walmart.com

On the question of treatment of employees, great-sounding policies don't mean much if you can't implement them universally across the organisation. Whether you like it or not, and however unfair it might be, 'a few bad apples' *can* ruin the whole barrel once the media or the courts get hold of the complaint.

Finally, if philanthropy could solve the image problem, then Wal-Mart, the US's biggest corporate donor, would be the US's most popular company. The good and bad news is that it's your core business that people worry about, not your good works.

The problem of corruption

It is an abiding mystery that the hard-headed, ball-busting, kick-ass (insert your own bizarre anatomical cliché here) business realists who take greatest pride in cutting costs and avoiding taxes are also the ones who take most pleasure in paying bribes. We can see him[34] now, leaning on a bar, beer in one hand and local girl in the other, relaxing after a hard day of screwing suppliers down to the last penny and concocting clever schemes with lawyers to declare all his taxable profits in the Gilbert and St Lewis islands. 'Corruption is just the way business is done here. There's no alternative', they weakly say, as they passively commit their shareholders to unnecessary costs and increased risk.

Perhaps there is some macho playground pleasure in breaking the rules, but we don't see why the rest of us should pay for it. So repeat after us. Corruption is a business cost that can be cut.

> ✎ As institutional investors with exposure to companies operating around the world, we believe it is in the interest of the companies in which we invest to operate in a business environment that is characterised by stability, transparency and respect for the rule of law. These factors are essential to securing economic prosperity and social cohesion, which, in turn, enable the companies in which we invest to prosper. However, they are frequently undermined by poor standards of governance and transparency, which can give rise to corrupt operating environments.
>
> We are concerned that extractive companies are particularly exposed to the risks posed by operating in these environments. Companies that make legitimate, but undisclosed, payments to governments may be accused of contributing to the conditions under which corruption can thrive. This is a significant business risk, making companies vulnerable to accusations of complicity in corrupt behaviour, impairing their local and global 'licence to operate', rendering them vulnerable to local conflict and insecurity, and possibly compromising their long-term commercial prospects in these markets.
>
> As institutional investors representing US$6.9 trillion (£3.8 trillion, €5.5 trillion), we actively support the development of international mechanisms

---

44   It *is* always a man.

to address payments transparency, and encourage other investors to join us in this statement.⁹⁹

Source: Payments Disclosure Group of Investors, 'Investors' Statement on Transparency in the Extractives Sector', February 2004; available at www.dfid.gov.uk/pubs/files/eitidraftreportinvestors.pdf.

⁶⁶The Bank has identified corruption as the single greatest obstacle to economic and social development. It undermines development by distorting the rule of law and weakening the institutional foundation on which economic growth depends.

The harmful effects of corruption are especially severe on the poor, who are hardest hit by economic decline, are most reliant on the provision of public services, and are least capable of paying the extra costs associated with bribery, fraud, and the misappropriation of economic privileges.⁹⁹

Source: World Bank website, www.worldbank.org/corruption

The difficulty with trying not to pay bribes is that it's an example of one of the most puzzling of conundrums—the **Prisoner's Dilemma**. If all businesses in a country refused to pay a bribe, then no bribes would ever be paid and people could continue to do business on equal terms without the extra cost and risk of corruption. Everyone except the corrupt recipient would be better off. But, for an individual business, the temptation is too strong. If no one else pays a bribe, then it makes sense to do so and get the contract. And, if everyone else is doing it, so should you or you'll be left at a disadvantage. So, regardless of what everyone else does, it pays to pay the bribe. Unfortunately, the same logic applies to everyone else, so everyone bribes. You're all back on the level playing field that you had when no one was paying a bribe, but in an environment of higher risk and higher cost.

The Prisoner's Dilemma

⁶⁶Tanya and Cinque have been arrested for robbing the Hibernia Savings Bank and placed in separate isolation cells. Both care much more about their personal freedom than about the welfare of their accomplice. A clever prosecutor makes the following offer to each. 'You may choose to confess or remain silent. If you confess and your accomplice remains silent I will drop all charges against you and use your testimony to ensure that your accomplice does serious time. Likewise, if your accomplice confesses while you remain silent, they will go free while you do the time. If you both

confess I get two convictions, but I'll see to it that you both get early parole. If you both remain silent, I'll have to settle for token sentences on firearms possession charges. If you wish to confess, you must leave a note with the jailer before my return tomorrow morning.'

The 'dilemma' faced by the prisoners here is that, whatever the other does, each is better off confessing than remaining silent. But the outcome obtained when both confess is worse for each than the outcome they would have obtained had both remained silent.["]

Source: Stanford Encyclopaedia of Philosophy (http://plato.stanford.edu/entries/prisoner-dilemma/, accessed 17 March 2006)

" **I can resist everything except temptation.**"

Source: Oscar Wilde, 'Lady Windermere's Fan'

We can learn here from an impressive organisation that has found a real-life solution to the real Prisoner's Dilemma—the mafia. By exerting an external force over the prisoners, it can change the rules of the game to its advantage. A prisoner will think: 'Of course I'm not going to confess—I don't want to wake up with a horse's head in my bed, my wife swimming with the fishes and my children propping up Brooklyn bridge in a concrete overcoat. And I know the other prisoner will feel the same. So I won't confess and neither will he. And he knows that too. So we're both better off.'

The existence of the mafia allows the prisoner to credibly promise to resist temptation and not confess. And importantly he knows the other prisoner faces exactly the same decision. It is an odd situation where the prisoner is helped by having a threat over his head and the existence of the mafia is an essential aid to mutual trust and prisoners' welfare. The system mostly works pretty well for the mafia. When it occasionally breaks down and the threats are no longer credible, informers become rife and the whole organisation falls apart, as the Prisoner's Dilemma once more wields its strange power.

The consortia that companies are beginning to use to combat corruption play a similar co-ordinating role that the mafia does for prisoners. Initiatives such as the Extractive Industries Transparency Initiative in oil and mining and the Kimberley Process in diamonds are all designed to help companies resist temptation, cut their costs and reduce their risk.

There are three crucial elements to such initiatives. The first is that it helps a member company to resist a demand for a bribe: 'I'm sorry I'd love to help but I can't. All our payments are transparent, we've made endless public commitments, and my chairman's been pictured shaking hands with Kofi Annan. We'd never get away with it.' Secondly, by joining together with other companies rather than making transparency a unilateral initiative, you can ensure that your competitors are subject to the same pressures and potential punishments and as a result you can all trust each other. Thirdly, it gives you the credibility, power and mutual protection to inform your local government when you're being pressured for bribes and when flaws in their regulatory systems encourage a culture of corruption. Temptation is resisted, solidarity is maintained and your costs are cut. The Prisoner's Dilemma has been defeated.

In a perfect world, it should be the job of the law to provide this sort of enforcement rather than rely on sector-specific initiatives organised by companies and NGOs. There is some evidence that the law, particularly in the USA, is getting stronger on these issues, but this is still far from clear-cut in practice (see the boxes for details). Like it or not, it is probably companies who will have to fill the enforcement gap.

Transparency International's Bribe Payers Index (BPI) and the OECD anti-bribery convention

❝ Just one in five of the respondents to the Gallup International poll across 15 leading emerging market economies is aware of the OECD Anti-Bribery Convention. The score is the same as in the first BPI in 1999.

Hailed as a landmark event, the ratification by the majority of leading industrial countries of the OECD Anti-Bribery Convention just over two years ago aimed to compel multinational firms to cease bribing foreign government officials by making such actions a criminal offence. The US was alone in having a similar law in place for more than two decades. 'According to the BPI data, the Convention does not seem to have made any difference, so far, to the bribery approaches of many multinational firms,' said Transparency International's Chairman Peter Eigen.

He noted that the first TI BPI in 1999 indicated that US firms, for example, were just as prone to using bribes abroad to win business as were German firms, which did not risk criminal prosecution for such actions and could set bribes abroad against their taxes. That survey also showed that only a very small percentage of overseas business executives, including representatives of Western multinationals, were informed about the Convention or had plans to enforce it. 'Today's new BPI data suggests that ignorance about the OECD Convention is widespread and that corporations clearly do not see the risks of criminal prosecution as particularly significant. This is a shocking conclusion.' **

Source: Transparency International Press Release, 14 May 2002.

** The surreal dilemmas sound like they could be drawn from a magazine advice column for paranoid lawyers: can I provide sacrificial goats for my customers in the Middle East? What if the client asks us to procure internal organs for his sick relative? Is it OK for me to donate cash at a Korean funeral?

These are not the made-up challenges of some legal agony aunt, but the real-life scenarios under discussion by senior executives responsible for setting policies for corporate hospitality and gifts in an increasingly strict US regulatory environment.

The conclusion of the executives, who recently gathered in New York for a summit on the problem, was that the fine grey line that separates acceptable generosity from the darker world of bribery and corruption has narrowed substantially. What lies behind their nervousness is the growing impact of Sarbanes–Oxley corporate governance legislation on the already strict rules of the US Foreign Corrupt Practices Act. Combine this with increasingly active enforcement agencies and the rapid globalisation of US business and there is a recipe for multinational angst on a grand scale.

Where minor local transgressions might once have been swept under the carpet, they are now likely to emerge as so-called 'material weaknesses' in internal control reports requiring sign-off from a chief executive and finance director worried about their own liability. What might be common practice in Seoul or Yemen may not look so wholesome in front of the Securities and Exchange Commission or a Manhattan jury. **

Source: Dan Roberts, *Financial Times*, 19 April 2005.

It appears that our hard-headed business realists have been missing out on the illicit pleasure of cutting costs by doing something really cunning. By co-operating with their competitors and the other international businesses in the country to resist the temptation of corruption, they can directly benefit at little or no cost. They'll be flooded with offers of help from governments, donor agencies and NGOs to help them organise and run the syndicate, they'll be contributing to development and they'll be strengthening the company's reputation. All it takes is convening power and the price of a few beers at the launch meeting. Worth a try?

In the 1980s, Huntsman Chemical opened a plant in Thailand. Mitsubishi was a partner in this joint venture, which we called HMT. With about $30 million invested, HMT announced the construction of a second site. I had a working relationship with the country's minister of finance, who never missed an opportunity to suggest it could be closer.

I went to his home for dinner one evening where he showed me 19 new Cadillacs parked in his garage, which he described as 'gifts' from foreign companies. I explained the Huntsman company didn't engage in that sort of thing, a fact he smilingly acknowledged.

Several months later, I received a call from the Mitsubishi executive in Tokyo responsible for Thailand operations. He stated HMT had to pay various government officials kickbacks annually to do business and that our share of this joint obligation was $250,000 for that year.

I said we had no intention of paying even five cents toward what was nothing more than extortion. He told me every company in Thailand paid these 'fees' in order to be guaranteed access to the industrial sites. As it turned out and without our knowledge, Mitsubishi had been paying our share up to this point as the cost of doing business, but had decided it was time Huntsman Chemical carried its own baggage.

The next day, I informed Mitsubishi we were selling our interest. After failing to talk me out of it, Mitsubishi paid us a discounted price for our interest in HMT. We lost about $3 million short term. Long haul, it was a blessing in disguise. When the Asian economic crisis came several years down the road, the entire industry went down the drain.

In America and Western Europe, we proclaim high standards when it comes to things such as paying bribes, but we don't always practice what we preach. Ethical decisions can be cumbersome and unprofitable in the near term, but after our refusal to pay 'fees' in Thailand became known, we never had a problem over bribes again in that part of the world. The word got out: Huntsman just says no. And so do many other companies.

Once you compromise your values by agreeing to bribes or payoffs, it is difficult ever to re-establish your reputation or credibility.

Source: Jon M. Huntsman, CEO Huntsman Chemicals, *Winners Never Cheat: Everyday Values We Learned as Children (But May Have Forgotten)* (Pennsylvania: Wharton School Publishing, 2005).

When Huntsman went public in early 2005, it had annual revenues exceeding $12 billion and major operations at 121 locations in 44 countries.

Follow-up questions

What is your Development Value Proposition? Is it reflected in your advertising and corporate communications? Do all of your staff understand it? Could you co-operate with local think-tanks to understand and communicate the value you create for the local economy?

Do you have a portfolio of supporters throughout the local community or are you reliant on one or two strong people? How confident are you in your ability to understand local politics? Could you 'outsource' your political concerns to local people?

Are you relying on temporary advantages based on market power or lack of regulation? How will you fare when the economy develops, regulation increases and competition gets tougher? Do you have plans to replace your temporary market power with sustainable competitive advantages?

Are you borrowing from and risking your parent company's reputation or are you adding to it? Do you understand the implications of new legislation such as the US Sarbanes–Oxley Act for your business? Are you missing opportunities to cut costs and risks by cutting corruption? Could you club together with other companies and donor-sponsored initiatives to reduce corruption and improve transparency?

Further reading

Winners Never Cheat: Everyday Values We Learned as Children (But May Have Forgotten) by Jon Huntsman, published by Wharton School Publishing (Pennsylvania) in 2005, gives a hard-headed and personal view of the importance of ethics and the strategic value of playing it straight.

The Prince of Wales International Business Leaders Forum (IBLF) sponsors a range of initiatives on corporate governance and economic development and will assist groups of companies to form coalitions to oppose corruption. Its website (www.iblf.org) offers a range of resources including case histories and sources of additional assistance.

Transparency International is the most prominent campaigner against corruption. Its website (www.transparency.org) offers a range of resources for free download, including Business Principles for Countering Bribery (BPCB). These are being used as the basis for anti-corruption criteria in the ethical investment index, FTSE4Good.

For links to these resources and other relevant material, go to www.makepovertybusiness.com.

10
Next steps

We normally read business books and, at the end, think: 'thanks very much. But what do you want us to actually *do*?' To try to avoid that trap, below we suggest some basic changes you could make to the way you do business in a developing country. As we said in Chapter 1, the final decisions on what initiatives you want to take can only rest with you—based on the details of your business and the details of the country you are in. But there are some general approaches you can take which will underpin your decisions and help you to implement them more effectively and at lower risk.

Find new sources of information

The key to coming up with new ideas is to have new information and new experiences. So develop a network of social contacts in the host community, development agencies, embassies, think-tanks and NGOs. Discuss the issues in this book with your staff, suppliers and customers, and encourage them to discuss with their families and friends. Encourage your staff to spend some time with poor people. Read your country's Poverty Reduction Strategy Paper.

If you want to go further, organise structured events at which staff, suppliers, customers, think-tanks and NGOs could invent and develop concrete project proposals that would implement some of the ideas in this book. You do not have to do it all yourself.

Understand the government's perspective

Whether you like it or not, government and business are closely intertwined in most developing countries. Ask the government what it wants from you and how you fit into their plan for the nation. Communicate what you contribute in technical ways that are relevant to their experts and in dramatic ways that are relevant to their politicians and the public. Write down your 'Development Value Proposition' and work out ways to defend it and develop it.

Analyse your own business

Ask yourself these questions:

- What are the elements of the business, economic, legal, and social infrastructure in your home country that you normally rely on to do business?
- What are the elements of the infrastructure that your customers normally rely on to do business with you?
- What's missing in your host country and how can you fill the gap?
- What partners could help you?
- What are their incentives?
- What are the barriers to local suppliers in doing business with you?
- What could you do by increased commitment to local supply?
- What training and information could you give?
- How could you share costs with other companies or with donors and NGOs?

Be cleverer about security

Discuss with your security experts how you can move from defending your location to securing your environment. Develop ideas to encourage the community to protect you. Assess whether your company is contributing to stability or instability, and ensure that your actions increase the gains from honest entrepreneurship and decrease the gains from violent activism or grabs for power. Discuss all this with the community, other companies, NGOs, donors and government.

Understand your relationship with your head office

Analyse and agree with head office what is fundamental about the business and what can be altered for local conditions. Identify why they have appointed you at all. Insulate yourself from head office pressures to make everything more complex and more expensive. Develop customer value propositions for your local market which can be transferred elsewhere in the company and ultimately back into home markets. Insist on a proper repatriation process when you return.

Prepare a migration plan

Prepare actions to deal with the fundamental country risk that economic development will make your business model redundant without you even noticing. Identify symptoms that this is already happening or will happen in the near future. Develop a strategy to localise your business and do not rely on artificial market power, weak regulation or corruption for your profits.

Forget the stereotypes

Not all poor people are helpless victims. Not all development activists are self-righteous gits. Remember that your strategic position is always strengthened when you widen the number of people you can deal with.

Correct us where we're wrong

Let us know which bits of this book are wrong. Tell donors, governments and NGOs what incentives and support you need to do better on development. This subject is wide open and nobody knows very much. Have a look at www.makepovertybusiness.com. Contribute to the debate.

Index

For Product Safety Concerns and Information please contact our EU
representative GPSR@taylorandfrancis.com
Taylor & Francis Verlag GmbH, Kaufingerstraße 24, 80331 München, Germany